The Death of Community Policing

OUR BROKEN JUDICIAL SYSTEM

COVER

**PC 384 Phil Schofield on his
Rubery Village Beat.
Photo taken c1985 by
PC 524 Brian Davies**

1

CONTENTS

Acknowledgements

Most books cannot be written without help from others. This book is no exception.

My grateful thanks go to Stuart Ind and Chris Munro, administrators of the Facebook site, 'West Mercia Memories' and the many members of it, too many to name, who contributed their memories to my many appeals for information.

I am also grateful to the numerous members of the Police History Society who similarly responded to my requests. But special thanks go to two members, Pam Mills M.A. and Terence Gardner who both managed to send me copies of the Home Office Circular 300/1944 which I have included in full in this book. That was the 'seed' planted which gave us our 'Residential Estate Beat Officers'. Pam also volunteered to 'beta read' my draft and as an author, gave me some excellent advice. She left the Kent Force as a Sergeant after 10 years' service to earn her master's degree in history and to raise her family. Terry Gardner is the secretary of the Warwickshire Police History Society. He retired as an Area Commander of the Special Constabulary with 28 years' service in the 'Specials'.

Front cover 'model' PC 384 Phil Scofield of West Mercia Police says, "It was my second spell as 'Rubery's Village Bobby' - I had started working Rubery a decade previously and it was certainly a challenge....Making conversation and contact with the public is (and always should be) the aim and purpose of Policing.

Thanks also to proof-readers, my neighbour Terence Westwood, a retired Surveyor and Building Engineer. He has worked for the last 20 years contributing updates and editing a technical looseleaf publication called Knights Guide to Building Control Law and Regulations (BREGS).

Also, Jim Jackson, a fellow member of Droitwich Golf Club.

Finally, my wife Jo who on every occasion I publish, asks me if this is the last book! She keeps putting up with me, but she might at last, have her way.

Introduction

I never really wanted to write this book having already written a similar one, 'The Changing Shapes of UK Policing'. That book merely identified the changes I recalled in my policing experience and not always what I considered to be the reasons for the changes made. In addition, there have been additional criticisms aimed at the police, but not only about the lack of professionalism displayed at incidents of crime, but also about the terrible criminal behaviour of some officers which has additionally caused the confidence and respect in the police to have taken a drastic downturn. They will never realise the harm they have caused to our already thin relationships with the community.

I am simply not the type of person who enjoys controversy, but I had had enough of the constant criticism aimed at the police which seemed to me to be ringing louder, more constantly and sometimes with added irrefutable evidence of their being a considerable drop in the effectiveness, efficiency and above all, the confidence in the police service, not least through that already mentioned above.

I was also concerned at how the police were being steered by the persuasiveness of non-police agencies, particularly those in the political shadowlands. In that context I am also not naive enough to fail to understand that I will inevitably be regarded as one of those ancient 'old dogs,' who are so out of date and unable to accept that evolution, by its very definition equates to changes. (Thank you David Hallmark)

So here I am, falling into the same mould as my older colleagues when I was a young copper. However, I do realise now, that circumstances surrounding us do change and that our actions may not always change in the best way to deal with those changes.

Including my cadetship, which commenced in 1960, I had completed 34 years' service when I retired as a chief superintendent. I had seen service on the beat as a constable on foot and in a panda car. As a detective, I had been a Sergeant, a Chief Inspector and a Superintendent. In that latter rank and as a Chief Superintendent, I had commanded two Divisions and the force

Operations Department in which I ran and expanded the force's Task Force. I was fully trained in Public Order Maintenance and a qualified Hostage Negotiator. Much of my time as a superintendent was engaged with anti-IRA measures, Royal and VIP visits, contingency planning and working on terrorism exercises.

On promotion to chief superintendent and whilst working with one of the five regional Her Majesty's Inspectors of Constabulary, John Woodcock [later Sir John], I had the privilege of examining the efficiency and effectiveness of nine different forces in England and Wales. However, by far the most important aspect of my policing career was that spent in the performance of what I call operational 'coal face' policing. This lasted for the whole of my service from the time I was attested in 1963 until I retired in November 1994 other than a short period as Deputy Commandant at our Force Training School and the longer periods spent behind a desk in the higher ranks when performing Sub Divisional and Divisional Commander roles.

Following my retirement, I became involved in a small project team rolling out the first computerised fingerprint storage, retrieval and search initiative in England and Wales. This involved me working closely with thirty-seven of the forty-three police forces in England and Wales. It also took me to the USA and in furtherance of an Interpol project, to most of the Caribbean Islands in order to build a 'proof of concept' pilot scheme to encourage the Islands to form a similar networked system.

I was then self-employed contracted to a French software company until February 2002. That gave me another eight years of policing experience albeit on foreign soil. In addition, I was also contracted as a para-legal with a number of Worcester UK solicitors and a high-profile firm of solicitors, 'Preston Gates' in Seattle, Washington USA.

In 2002 I was asked to enrol into a new scheme promoted by my old force, West Mercia Constabulary, in what was known as 'The Retained Experienced Personnel' scheme (REPs). We were just a handful of retired experienced officers who mostly had carried ranks from detective inspector to chief superintendent. Some were totally involved in statement taking and others in the mentoring of young officers and assisting in the crime investigations delegated to them. This was at a time when the force had begun making use of personal computers which were to be linked with on-the- ground policing and crime investigations.

One of my main tasks was to use my computer literacy to examine the crime recording, investigation and supervision of crime enquiries which were all logged on a 'paper free' new computer intranet system. I was shocked when I discovered that their crime investigations and more importantly, the supervision of them were sadly lacking. Things were so bad that on odd occasions, I accompanied probationer PCs on actual crime enquiries.

I also worked on 'cold case' murder investigations, and I designed and built intelligence packs for over 30 suspects involved in the world-wide child pornography investigation, 'Operation Ore'. I was also contracted separately to restructure West Mercia Police's organisation of its 'Personal Standards' departments over the force area when the process of complaints against the police was changed from the Police Complaints Authority to The Independent Police Complaints Commission.

I also received separate contracts from the then deputy chief constable regarding the administration of delicate discipline investigations. It was during this period that I was able to automatically 'catch up' on what had been happening in the police service during those eight years I had been otherwise occupied at home and abroad.

So, with this forty-six years police experience, I realised that I had achieved quite a broad policing experience. In fact, so far as general police work is concerned, it probably represented one of the broadest policing experiences one could gather. As a genealogist and a social historian, if I were not to record them as I have done here, the opportunity to place my findings on record would be lost forever.

I, therefore, regard this current book as more of a 'Social History' document tracing some 'pros and cons' of the evolution of police work. I must therefore, apologise to those in the West Mercia Police Force who, only because I have gained most of my experience in it and live in the area, will take the brunt of my criticisms. I am sure that the same level of 'bumps in the road', will be found in most, if not in all other English and Welsh forces. My grumbles, therefore, are not with individuals, but with the system and the leaders of this new policing era. The influences of these, I have learned, have spread nationwide and have led to my belief that many of the desired leadership qualities worked under have now diminished or are totally missing.

1. The Queen Died Yesterday

The Queen died yesterday, 8th September 2022. I could not help wondering if, compared with era's past, she would have been aware of the true state of her realm in so far as the degree of her subjects' morals, respect, and criminality, were concerned. There appears to me, to be a considerable increase in our population's criminality and the failure to report it. This coupled with the police's inability to tackle it, especially knife crime, sexual attacks, public disorder, drugs abuse and 'online' frauds. This also unfortunately coincides with the absence of visible policing and the respect and confidence once held in them by the communities they policed. Would the Queen have believed as I do, that such behaviour has slipped and continues to slip as time passes us by?

So, this was the day which tipped me over the edge to start writing again after I had promised myself (and my wife) that I would abstain. The views proffered in the chapters that follow are, unless stated, well and truly my own and that I am fully aware that others will not agree with them.

Over the ensuing period of the Queen lying in state, we witnessed thousands of people paying their respects. The whole period of mourning appeared to me to have had at least a tiny effect on the restoration of humanity in our communities, but it left me wondering how long that will last. One thing I am sure about is that the people who paid their respects to her in those queues would not have been the type of people the police have to deal with daily. They would not include those who inflict pain and harm to others by taking up offensive weapons with intent to do harm or deal in prohibited drugs, and those who wish to steal from their fellow subjects, or indeed those fraudsters who want to hack into other people's computers whether just for fun or to defraud them.

It appears to me that all these forementioned 'types' are on the increase and that the general respect for other people and their property has waned, so why would they have respect for their Queen? I am sure that she would have been aware that her sovereign role would not include her getting embroiled in such debate and thus, she would have been far too diplomatic to become involved. However, she has not been confined in a cocoon and would have been fully aware of media edicts about such issues. By the same tone, I would not be surprised if she had dropped little hints to the gaggle of prime ministers, she met during their many audiences with her. Perhaps we shall never know and it is better that we do not.

Many will say that not much has changed during her long reign, but those changes have been apparent for some time. They may rightly say that such modern-day facilities and communications have merely served to magnify these perceptions, thus appearing to cast them in an increasingly worsening light. Whilst that maybe so, now that I have reached the grand old age of 78 and, unlike many who are now influencing the practice and procedures of policing today, I have been fortunate to have been positioned to be able to draw comparisons. This is not only in the organisation and structure of policing, but also in the changes of human social behaviour. I conclude that the qualities I have mentioned above, are slowly diminishing, and are not now held in such high esteem.

So, what on earth has happened to our beloved country, its population and political leaders, in what appears to me, to be over such a short period of time? I truly believe that 2022 was the culmination of around 30 years of pussy footing around with more effort being expended into such subjects as inclusion, diversity (with racism and sexism at the helm), misogyny, health and safety, data protection, human rights and everything else wrapped up into what these days, I am led to believe to be classified as 'Wokism', whatever that means. But do not think for a second, that I believe those subjects are not important; to the contrary, I feel a sickness in my stomach when I read about the behaviour of some of my past colleagues. This is a feeling appearing to be getting more rampant as time passes. My feelings, however, are that when addressing these problems, we should not lose sight of our core objectives and it is that, which I believe has occurred.

If I am correct in that respect, I believe that the problem must lie with force management teams who, with little or no experience of community policing, but who often now employ expensive assistance to produce reams of what I call, 'gobbledegook' in personnel matters and those issues which I have described above as 'Wokism'. The worst part of all this from my point of view is that most have been restrained from proffering such views for fear of being outcast as non-politically correct. Good police management and leadership ought to result in the automatic correction of any wrongdoing or mismanagement without such expensive and 'overkill' measures which must only detract from core policing objectives.

In my view, and I realise this will be hotly contested, we have witnessed far too many appointments resulting from reversed discrimination just to satisfy the ethos of inclusion. It should always be 'the right person for the job', no matter of what race, gender, creed or colour – Full Stop! I shall return to this subject later.

During the months of September and October 2022, we lived under the Prime Ministership of three Prime Ministers in rapid succession! Am I the only one thinking that each one of them did not have the qualities of leadership expected of such responsible positions? Could this situation in itself, be a reflection of the diluted managerial levels across the whole spectrum of business and commerce issues? Welcome to the 'Wokeshire Constabulary or the 'Hot Potato' era where important jobs and responsibilities are hastily passed on to fewer suspecting recipients.

As if to add weight to my beliefs, my barometer which measures police effectiveness has recently dived after I recently studied the report on the aftermath of the 2017 Manchester Arena disaster (yes, that was five years ago!) where maybe, people were scared to act without fear of criticism. (My belief, but suspicions only) It appears that the emergency services involved – British Transport Police, Greater Manchester Police, Ambulance Service and Fire and Rescue Service, were not acting in unison to achieve the overall objective of saving life. The Gold, Silver and Bronze commanders were not getting together and, in some instances, some had not even realised that they were holding such key positions. "Lessons will be learned" is NOT a phrase that can be used here. All these lessons had already been learned but once again, they had not been utilised. I wonder if the appropriate training had been given. Why else were all the emergency services stood back while those both injured and uninjured did their incompetent best to assist the dying and more seriously injured whilst those so called 'leaders' of the various emergency services involved, were passing the 'hot potato' or refusing to let the personnel under their command free to provide the assistance they had been trained for and were paid to provide?

Bold statements to make on my behalf I know, but I cannot believe that all those firefighters, ambulance and police personnel were not straining at the bit to get in there and save lives. It appears to me that they had not been 'switched on' by their poor leadership. Surely 'Risk Assessments' were not involved but as the stories now spread over our newspapers, maybe they were. The media have been shouting such terms as 'INSTITUTIONAL COWARDICE'! I do not believe that to be true for one second. As stated above, those at the coal face must surely have been willing and eager to get in there and help. So, who or what was it that was holding them back? The report makes horrific reading.

I believe that it is today's leadership or their skills of management whether in the police or elsewhere which are now on trial. In the operational sense, that will include the so-called gold, silver and bronze commanders employed from top to bottom who make the operational decisions in such instances. I can only speak for the police, but I guess the same practices apply in all emergency services. Having been in those command roles and realise that there are many times when important decisions need to be made and made very quickly, sometimes instinctively. No time to get the books out etc. I was always told that we should do as we think should be done in the circumstances.

It seems like every day popular newspapers carry headlines questioning the lack of police decisiveness. One that I have recently experienced asks, WHAT IS THE POINT OF THESE POLICE? This accompanied a photograph of a 'Just Stop Oil' protestor who had climbed onto a gantry of the M25 motorway. Beneath him many police vehicles are parked up and police officer are gazing up at him. Meanwhile, the M25 motorway became seized with frustrated drivers praying that the demonstrator would fall or be dragged off so that they could get on with their business.

What the newspapers do not point out is that since the days of my 'Old School' policing, the laws have changed. They always have done through a series of High Court stated cases from which evolves our 'Common Law', which carries as much weight as our 'Statute Law'. I read that many of the recently made 'Case Laws' now include a more severe peppering of 'human rights' considerations which would affect decisions in the Courts of Appeal. Impinging on our human rights to protest may well result in convictions being quashed by the appeal courts, the Supreme Court in particular. Some conclude that the Police may therefore be wasting their time and money to make arrests.

Maybe it is this reasoning which has caused Chief Constable Chris Noble who leads the National Police Chiefs Council (NPCC) on tackling protests, to defy the Home Secretary's directive to crackdown on what they call 'these disruptive eco-zealots'. He is quoted to have said, "We're not going to arrest our way out of environmental protests". With a sound record of policing stemming from that with the Police Service of Northern Ireland, it appears that the considerations of these frustrated drivers, have now taken a back seat in his considerations. He does not now sound like a leader of most of the police officers that I once worked with, but could it be that is the line he is now forced down by leaders in other higher places?

But of course, unlike those chiefs I worked with, he and his colleagues now work under different conditions and under fixed term contracts. We no longer hear chief officers remonstrating with edicts produced by the Home Office, often in my opinion, without common sense. With mostly placed political appointments above them in the form of Police and Crime Commissioners, they need to act accordingly to keep their jobs.

To arrest anyone obstructing busy motorways or elsewhere, is a serious action which can blight a person's future for life. Whether a person should be arrested or not or whether any particular action taken, is a good example of the dilemma now faced by chief officers. It was always impressed upon me during my early training that "If you think that the person, you are dealing with ought to be arrested, then arrest him or her"!! "You will always be supported" was the added advice, even though it might transpire later that no power of arrest then existed: but the decisions were honourable and would receive support.

But is that notion now viable? Maybe we should first examine what happened at Hillsborough on Saturday April 15th, 1989. Could that have also caused a different breed of chief officer who would be resistant now in the taking of any action which might affect their own and their family's lives for ever?

David Duckenfield was freshly promoted to chief superintendent just 19 days before the Hillsborough disaster. He had been blessed (or cursed) with being the 'Police Match Commander' of that day. As an aside, being a chief superintendent meant that he would not be paid for doing that job. It was a Saturday and chief superintendents were not paid for any overtime worked. (In my day anyway!) If he had been lucky, he may have later taken a day off in lieu. As it happened, this must have been the worst day in his life and being paid or not, would have been immaterial. When putting his uniform on during that morning, he would never have dreamt how his life was about to change for ever. I do not want to get embroiled in pointing fingers here again, as we know that the police have shouldered the blame for mistakes made and although I believe that some supporters contributed to the disaster, police action played an important part, and I am never going to duck that.

I obviously feel for all those 96 people who lost their lives that day and their families, but I have to admit some sympathy towards David Duckenfield who looked a broken man on leaving court. His punishment had been served during all those 30 odd years waiting for his fate. – Yes, I know that he is still alive, and 96 supporters are not, but I bet the life he has lived since has been like a living death.

He and Bernard Murray his deputy and a more experienced match commander, had both been charged with various offences which boiled down to causing these deaths and in addition, they were charged under the Police Discipline Regulations for 'Neglect of Duty'. They were never going to end their careers as 99.99% of other officers would. The 'hot potato' had been handed to them and their fingers scalded. Bernard Murray was close to tears when he told the jury: "I feel a great deal of sympathy and sadness for the people who I

14

have seen here every day. "I am a parent myself and I know what they have lost. I know how they must feel, and I know that a lot of them must blame me . . . I do feel a sense of responsibility and always have. I do feel very sorry for their loss." He was to die of cancer a few years later. Both had suffered post-traumatic stress disorder.

It was not until November 2019 that David Duckenfield was eventually cleared of the manslaughter charge he faced. Although a broken man, I fully realise that no sympathy at all for their 30 years of anguish would be shed by any Liverpool Football Club fan and of course, none would be expected especially from those related to those killed. Opening the gate might have saved lives – it might have done – but the coin fell on the wrong side, and it caused lives to be lost by those rushing in all being channelled into the same direction, thus killing those innocent soles lower down nearer to the perimeter fence. The disaster happened and once again, hindsight proved that it is a remarkable skill!

This book is not about that at all. I reiterate it here to emphasise how our police responsibilities have evolved to weighing far heavier on existing shoulders, and, to what consequence that might have had at subsequent disasters, such as was witnessed at the Manchester arena.

£60m, five separate jury court cases, thirty years and still NO ONE is found responsible for unlawful killing of 96 football fans at Hillsborough

- David Duckenfield was police match commander at the Hillsborough disaster
- He went on trial for gross negligence manslaughter over the deaths of fans
- Following a retrial, he was cleared today, prompting anger among relatives

Mail on Line – 28th November 2019

I wonder now whether chief constables and other Gold Commanders are thinking twice about making decisions which they could pay for, for the rest of their lives. This is evolution and I wonder whether that could have been the start of some reluctance by so called leaders, to 'jump in' where angels feared to tread? I cannot believe that could have caused policies to have flown from some office bound 'job's worth' who had not the nerve to support the immediate action which so obviously was required to be taken at Manchester? Has there been some, who possibly to save their own back and without having the experience of dealing with such issues, have decreed that a 'Risk Assessment' must be made in such circumstances which will preclude immediate assistance being provided to those in need of their help'. **I DO NOT KNOW BUT I JUST HOPE THAT I'M WRONG**. Believe you me, there is no time to even find the pen with which to write a risk assessment!

It is the heroes of this world who when asked, "Didn't you think of the dangers involved?" invariably reply that they did not. They just acted on the spur of the moment and got on with their job. Sometimes that is necessary.

If I am correct in the belief that the police no longer appear to act in haste and with the fervour which I had witnessed and experienced during my long association with the police, then can it be a coincidence that all my negative observations seem to run alongside each other in tandem with all this unexplainable plague of 'Wokism' which has so quickly infected the land we love?

Our forces now comprise a completely new set of people who appear to be placing 'human rights' issues on a much higher priority than simply tackling the cause of problems faced. Yes, they must be fully cognisant of our rights but in the knowledge that they only police with their community's consent and thus with its support, surely in the M25 example, they should arrest them, clear the carriageway and let those arrested, go through the justice system which may well entail convictions being quashed. The outcome is not a matter for police debate at the scene, that should, as I say, be left to others. So far as I am aware, it is still an offence to obstruct the highway and police commanders should lead and not cow down to those in ivory towers who do not have as much policing nous as themselves.

Do not misunderstand me, I would have, or will gladly led a law-abiding protest anytime, but I am left wondering how much carbon was spat out by those stationery vehicles and how many millions of pounds did that protest cost our economy and the occupants of those stuck there wondering why the police weren't doing their job in clearing the carriageways. I raise this subject of 'Human Rights' here because what is so plainly obvious to me, is the high level of persuasion and degree to which its ethos has now been applied to ensuring the adherence of them in all aspects of policing. That is not to say that they should, in any way be ignored, but I contend that their application to everyday policing seems to me, to be a giant overkill, to such extents that forces have applied so much 'gobbledegook' about it in general. Much of the strategy being delivered by the 'top landings' at most police forces, has been fed down from on high by such bodies as The College of Policing and The National Police Chief Council (NPCC). The policy of Diversity, Equality and Inclusion strategy (DEI) is a good example which I would wager without any evidence at all, has probably been promulgated by the government through the auspices of the Home Office and their 'think tanks'.

This will be discussed further at Chapter five where I provide a taste of what such documents include but for now, below is just the heading attributed to it by West Mercia Police. The Foreword and the Introduction will provide a taste of the 'gobbledegook' and the overuse of 'buzz words' I discuss later in Chapter five.

I am afraid that such documents convey to me that "This is what we've been told to do, and we shall do it!". If that is so, tell the public in the media and broadcast it. In other words, be as transparent as you say you will be in your published objectives, do not cow down. However, having been raised among the police family, although the objective is written in gobbledegook, there are obviously threads in it that I understand but I wonder who it is that these types of documents are aimed at? I have only produced below, the paragraphs which relate to the **'workforce'** as is contained in the actual Diversity, Equality and Inclusion Strategy. It read as follows: -

Engagement with our talented workforce is just as important, ensuring we establish a fair, flexible and inclusive culture which fosters well-being and which allows us to attract and retain a truly diverse pool of officers and staff. These aspirations are set out in our People Strategy, which is driven by our force vision, values and priorities.

*Under the heading, '**What factors have informed our Strategy and equality objectives?***

- *Workforce composition (equality) data over a 5-year period in relation to protected characteristics, by rank and grades.*

- *Feedback and insight from accountability and performance reviews with the Police and Crime Commissioner which have helped identify workforce themes and patterns we need to address.*

- *It seeks to put in place mechanisms that ensure we embed diversity, equality and inclusion in all aspects of our decision-making, policy and practice, creating and retaining an engaged workforce that is representative of those diverse communities we serve.*

- *Furthermore, the purpose of this strategy is to help us to continue to be proactive in identifying and removing barriers to inclusion and equality both in our workforce and in the wider community. It supports us to work in partnership with other agencies. It guides the actions and initiatives that allow us to comply with our duties under the Equality Act 2010.*

Under the heading 'Organisation': -

- ***Transparency and scrutiny:*** *We will make our organisation as transparent as possible and encourage scrutiny of our activities by*

Staff Networks, Independent Advisory Groups and other stakeholders. We will ensure that through this greater involvement how we have responded to feedback to improve our service. We will publish required equality data.

- **Developing our workforce:** *We will develop all our officers and staff so that they have a strong awareness of how equality, diversity and inclusion supports us to achieve a positive, dynamic working culture and a truly effective police service.*

- **Understanding our workforce:** *We will improve our understanding of the makeup of our workforce by putting systems in place to better analyse equality addressing any under-representation or disproportionality through innovative recruitment, retention and progression strategies. We will engage and involve the workforce in embedding inclusive practices.*

- *We will involve the workforce in the revision of policies, guidance and support related to equality, diversity and inclusion, including the reporting of inappropriate or discriminatory behaviour, working with a cross-section of teams in a 'Speak Up' group to facilitate and monitor the effectiveness of this.*

- *Our Strategic decision-making, Governance and Delivery Boards for workforce and policing issues will have a requirement that the equality and inclusion impacts of decisions have been considered.*

- *We will continue to enhance systems to improve the collection and analysis of workforce equality data (protected characteristics) at recruitment and at all stages of the employment cycle so that we can better identify and develop strategies to address under representation, disproportionality or unfairness and ensure our welfare and employee support services acknowledge and meet diverse needs in relation to protected characteristics.*

- *We will continue to listen carefully to the experiences of our workforce through staff surveys, focus groups and consultation to address inequalities. Themes emerging from consultation have informed our delivery plans for our People Strategy and DEI work. We will report on outcomes.*

- *We will develop and deliver our recruitment, retention and progression plans to build a representative workforce which offers everyone equality of opportunity to progress and flourish. (We have detailed plans to support these areas of our work, including our 'Step In, Step Up and Step across programmes).*

- *We will introduce and embed Equality Standards benchmarking tools to measure and improve our DEI performance & outcomes against evidenced good practice in other forces and other sectors, consulting and reporting with transparency on our progress and action plans with our workforce.*

- *We will devise learning and development plans for diversity and set agreed learning outcomes. People will be supported to set performance objectives for diversity, equality and inclusion which are applicable to their roles and have clarity on their rights and responsibilities in relation to taking forward duties under the Equality Act and our Code of Ethics.*

  Currently, our workforce data shows that we are under-represented in terms of Black, Asian and Minority Ethnic officers and staff, particularly at senior grades. We are also under-represented in terms of women at senior levels. Please note, 2021 census data will impact on our understanding of levels of proportionate representation.

- *We are focussing on attracting a diverse workforce in terms of all protected characteristics. Before setting aspirations for protected characteristics such as disability or sexual orientation, for example, we are undertaking work to address non-disclosure within the workforce.*

- *BAME (Black Asian and Minority Ethnic) has been an overarching term used in policing and other sectors to refer to ethnic groups which have typically been under-represented in the workforce and to support the monitoring of diversity and inclusion. The government has issued guidance (2021) on the preferred term 'ethnic minorities' to now refer to all ethnic groups except*
the White British group. Ethnic minorities include White minorities, such as Gypsy, Roma and Irish Traveller. We will continue to consult with our workforce and communities on their preferred terminology when discussing issues of inclusion, representation or disparity. The Government uses 18 standardised ethnic groups to analyse and monitor ethnicity data.

Did you manage to read every word? I can hear the comedian Catherine Tate dressed up as her grandmother exclaiming, "What the f--- is all that about"?

I cannot believe that such gobbledegook is required in such a modern policing organisation. It has clearly been written with assistance (more likely totally) from those highly qualified in such 'Human Resources' matters. I would go as far as to suggest that it is all part of the defence mechanisms knee jerked into such strategies from the edicts of those at a higher level and who know very little about policing and those who police. They may well have issued this 'dripped down' ammunition through the NPCC, the College of Policing and to Chief Officers of Police who appear to me, to have placed a far heavier resource than is required and above all, ahead of their primary and fundamental objectives which they swore to uphold when they were attested. That attestation being sworn by all recruits contains sufficient to remind them how they should carry out their duties. If they do not do so, then they may be disciplined on such a scale that the message would be driven home.

2. What the Heck Has Been Going On?

I have written many thousands of words in an aura of being perplexed at what comes to my senses when, on almost a daily basis, I absorb instances in the media which I can only describe as involving policing 'shambles'. I shall recount some below. So, I am not only now curious at what Her Majesty may have been wondering about our state of affairs, but now surely, most of our law-abiding citizens will also be scratching their heads?

I have reviewed, surveyed, questioned, and even raised the subject on the last Tuesday of each month at The Wheatsheaf pub, Fromes Hill on the borders of Herefordshire and Worcestershire where a sadly reducing small number of retired 'Old School' superintendents and chief superintendents meet for lunch. We exchange notes on our prescribed medication, along with those 'glory' stories of yesteryear which we have heard over and over and over again. Yep, I have to concede that apart from us all re-joining as a 'Dad's Army' to put the wheels back on, not even that forum has come up with a sensible answer, nor, I would add, in reality would our 'Dad's Army'.

Those who know me will vouch that all my hair has gone – pulled from the roots and the scalp scratched to death with bewilderment. Just how can a police service change so quickly even if it has taken around 30 years – that is a very rapid transformation when considering what has gone on in the annals of police history since Robert Peel gave birth to policing in 1829.

I want to make it very clear again from the outset, that I apportion no blame whatsoever on the individual boys and girls who join the force today or indeed, the current leaders of our police who without exception, were not in the police service to experience what real community policing was all about. I feel it is the new 'regime' now evolving from those leaders at the Home Office, the academia of police studies and the profession of policing itself through the National Police Chiefs Council, the College of Policing and the Police Inspectorate, right down to the lack of experienced operators and leaders at

Community policing level. Through no fault of their own, they were born too late not to be so employed when 'Community Policing' died and therefore have no experience of it. Without a great deal of eating humble pie and a willingness to learn from the past, it will take giant leaps of faith and a huge amount of courage to get us back on the tracks of the most effective methods of policing so that a firm platform can be utilised to work in conjunction with the more modern tools contained in today's policing armoury.

I am not that stupid to even think that we can return to the policing of the past but if I can get acknowledged a tiny fraction of how and why it evolved at least after the last war, then those in power today, might be able to tweak their objectives at least towards the concepts that worked very well in a preventive mode which, due to our reliance on responsive policing, has now disappeared. You cannot measure prevention; you can measure crime increase and decrease but you cannot measure how many crimes were prevented by a visible police presence and this may have influenced the judgement of the Police Scientific and Research Department in c1967 when they took police officers off the beat to drive motor vehicles. I contend that they did not understand the value of community 'preventive' policing.

Many of the changes we've witnessed have been cost cutting measures, possibly arrived at due to the extra budgetary requirements demanded of the addition of such agencies as Crown Prosecutors and Police and Crime Commissioners, both Government led ideas. We have sold off millions of pounds worth of police houses and police stations, but it is nigh impossible to arrive at a definitive appreciation of the effect that has had. The cupboard is now bare, and I firmly believe that the absence of visible neighbourhood policing has a great deal to do with a public lack of respect and confidence in the police and escalating crime and public order trends.

My retirement was too many years ago for anyone to take my comments here too seriously, but due to the jobs I was employed in, I was not so close to the troops on the ground as I had been in the past. My job as head of the Operations Department, did not entail that responsibility for the day-to-day 'mothering' of the many personnel on shifts and departments under my wing as it had in other posts. I was, for the main, deploying, and orchestrating plans and officers who belonged beneath the wings of other commanders, not my own wings.

Fate had played its hand and after staying on for a while, I retired and fell into a great position being kept busy all over the UK, the USA and later, the Caribbean Islands working on the digital fingerprint recording and searching initiative which I have already explained in the 'Introduction'. I guess I had become so completely oblivious of the gradual but continual decline in behaviour and criminality which appeared to have hit communities during my period of absence. (Not that my absence had in any way, contributed!!)

On reflection, in addition to some changes made in the late 1980s which I shall explain below, this 1994 period commencing my retirement, probably helped to sound the death knell of 'The Old School' and heralded the first steps towards the arrival of the more modern 'Wokeshire Constabulary'.

I shall contend in the chapters that follow, that the Force, Constabulary or Police Service had been 'RE-SET' in many ways. In short, there had been a massive change in policing and the culture of its recruits entering the service just after I retired. In the 'old school' era, it had been very difficult to find recruits to join 'THE JOB'. When found, if you were the right size and could pass simple educational tests, you were in. In my case, if they believed you could represent the force well at football, rugby, or cricket, then maybe you could get in any way!

Apart from many ex-servicemen looking for the police accommodation on offer or a rent allowance in lieu, we had recruited from farm labourers, electricians, plumbers, warehousemen and tradesmen from the building industry. There were also the administrative types, – the ones that could read and write to standards probably just above the average. There were also butchers, shop assistants, sales reps, miners from Wales and Derbyshire and many others which if all were put into that great big melting pot, would represent a desired 'microcosm of society'.

By now it was recognised that we could do with more graduates in the higher ranks. I have never argued against that because I could recall some great leaders in my time of an ilk that doesn't seem to be present nowadays. During my latter days, some possessed degrees but there were some that didn't, but would call a spade a spade and had been 'at the coal face' themselves. We needed to be sure to retain the thief catchers and general worker bees who were happy policing in the lower ranks and with a good helping of common sense.

These were the days when among all this variety of skills, policing skills, in one form or another would automatically surface. There were many who were hell bent on driving, and so, the Traffic Division always had a long waiting list. Thief catchers automatically identified themselves as they were more frequently bringing prisoners arrested into the 'charge office'. As an example, I recall that Tony Barnes (Barney) had a phenomenal arrest record. We called him a 'jammy bugger' until we realised that on lates and nights shifts, he would secret himself in one of the coaches owned by a company, 'Bounds', which were parked up in a line at the back of the bus station car park. They were always left unlocked! He had got himself a grandstand view in the warm and dry of his beat which overlooked all those cars parked up by cinema goers who were at the nearby Ritz cinema. To make it easier for thieves to break into these cars, there were no lights within the car park and of course, the thieves would know what time their car owners would be leaving the cinema. This situation was 'manna from heaven' for thieves and for Barney, and he was blessed with arrest after arrest. Doing the paper work was not the easy part for him but in those days, it was the arrests that mattered and there was always someone better educated who could help him out with the admin. Barney and many other good coppers would never be able to join the force today. (Neither would I) He would have few, if any educational qualifications, certainly no degree nor would he in a month of Sundays agree to studying for one as an apprentice; as is advertised today.

So that was how CID officers were identified. If you were a good thief catcher, you might be lucky and be able to claim one of the very limited places available in the CID. Competition was exceedingly high. When as a detective chief inspector (DCI), I recall PC Harold Farmer who was itching to become a detective. He would plague me verbally and on paper but there simply was no vacancies, he would have been good at it but sadly he never made it as he was killed in a road accident or road collision.

Arresting criminals was what it was all about – even the Traffic cars had their shift league tables and they often bragged that they could catch more criminals than the CID. The rest of us posted to city beat patrols were hell bent on making more arrest on nights than those on the other shifts. I would climb the fire escapes at the back of large business premises and hotels, have a smoke, sit and listened. It paid off but the results were very much like my fishing. Not always productive but when they were, by God what a buzz that gave.

It was in this era of the 1960s and with such competition existing that maybe the wheel started to buckle. The identity of burglars and thieves would invariably be known through the network of informants and the like. We could not reach the successes to such a high level without detective officers who could cultivate and speak the language of their informants. There were always a few rogue families who were responsible for most of the crimes. But without the evidence, many of them had been through the mill so often that they would simply smile and deny any wrongdoing. It was probably this era that brought those nasty headlines to notice when police were accused of planting evidence and obtaining admissions by any means. 'Verballing', which credited thieves with making admissions which they had not fully made, was another of the 'bent' cards alleged to have been played. They may have been 'nasty' headlines but they were required. I have no doubt that they were true, but not in anything like the proportions being alleged. We have always suffered the 'tar brush' particularly concerning the corruption which had been identified in the larger 'Metropolitan' type forces, and London's Met. Police were very often those on the starting line. We have a lot NOT to thank those forces for.

Those as old as I will remember the 1970s when Sir Robert Mark was appointed the Commissioner of the Met. He was determined to get to the root cause of the problem and during his term, 478 officers left the force concerning criminal or disciplinary proceedings. In his book, "In the Office of Constable' he wrote that in thirty years working in provincial forces he "had never experienced institutionalised wrongdoing, blindness, arrogance and prejudice on anything like the scale accepted as routine in the Met". He called a meeting of representatives of the CID and "told them they represented what had long been the most routinely corrupt organisation in London". The corruption which then existed gave birth to the term 'Noble Cause'. This was to mean that false evidence which was thought to justify the ends. The problem was laid at the feet of the CID which was integrated with the rest of the service at all levels; they were no longer able to conduct their own disciplinary investigations or arrange their own promotions. However, Sir Robert also said,

"...it cannot be over emphasized that notwithstanding its defects, it (the CID) always contained a considerable number of thoroughly honest, dedicated and skilled detectives at every level...".

As if wanting to balance the situation even more, he commented that the system of justice was weighted so heavily in favour of the criminal and the defence lawyers that it could only be made to work by bending the rules. Little did he know that that situation was to become even more restricting in years to come.

It is widely accepted that it was Sir Robert's work that went a long way towards the implementation of legislation such as The Police and Criminal Evidence Act 1984 (PACE) which in effect, stopped malpractice and transformed the processes involved in the treatment of suspects.

There were cases elsewhere; I recall Leeds officers using rhino whips on their suspects in custody but by and large, most of the preventive measures introduced have, in my opinion been because of the sizes of such huge forces, primarily the Metropolitan force which, again in my opinion, cannot be controlled by one person at the top of the tree. Whilst I fully realise that that person will have a myriad of support at that level, I am on record in my belief that the Met. together with the City of London Police, should be disbanded and merged into the existing London home county forces. That being so, there would be no reason why support and personnel functions could not be operated in a 'regionalised' basis so as not to duplicate them.

So, having got that off my chest, although rumours will always be told and heard, I can place my hand on my heart and swear that I had never any experience myself or knowledge of others getting up to such things, but I shall explain more on this subject later on.

Compared with the Met, most other county forces comprised backwater rural 'family type' forces and, so far as I was aware, such things would not have been expected to have happened in those forces, at least to any like level. To the contrary, I was often in awe when witnessing the way admissions were obtained by seasoned CID officers who were very highly skilled in the way they interviewed suspects. They had no need to be violent, bang the desk or induce fear in any way. I hoped to develop such skills myself, but it took me years of practice until I felt a warm of satisfaction when obtaining such confessions.

Of course, we had the Judges Rules to contend with. These were guidance notes which although not wrapped in legislation, were defined to protect persons in custody and heaven help those who were found out to have broken them. It is here that maybe I can plead guilty to minor misdemeanours but then so could just about everyone else, although that of course, is no excuse.

It should be remembered that we interviewed suspects without being tape recorded or filmed. What was said and recorded on paper was a matter for those in the interview room, or more likely, the officer deputed to do the writing. In that context, I challenge anyone to record contemporaneously, what was asked of the suspect and the replies that were given. As one might expect, a confession might well have been the result of a long and more rapid exchange of questions and answers and I could not swear that all of the conversations were recorded in writing. So long as the confession was made and it meant the same as the proverbial, "Ok Guv. It's a fair cop, I did it" is included, it mattered not if the conversation was abbreviated, or actually verbatim, so long as it conveyed what was actually meant.

The problem remained that in cases which were denied, there would always be the clever ones that shaded the conversations toward guilt rather than the exact words. This so-called 'verballing' would be included in that definition of 'Noble Cause' malpractice. It was also against the Judges Rules to make promises to the future to suspects. I could sign up to having broken that rule many times but normally out of kindness. However, if a promise was made, then it would be kept. Suspects often believed that they might be remanded in custody when it was known that they would receive police bail. Maybe I promised that "I would do what I could" – I never broke those promises except that they should not have been made in the first place, most would be getting bail no matter what.

Inevitably, borderline acceptable benchmarks of wrongdoing shifted in the wrong direction by the most unscrupulous and it must be said that some innocent persons might have been dragged into the net, though as far as I am aware, I would doubt very much that they did in Herefordshire or West Mercia at least.

It was inevitable that with the degree that such corruption had spread within the Met, something like a huge sledgehammer was then on the drawing board and the rest of us small 'nuts' were about to be cracked. But of course, this messing around trying to extract confessions by questionable means had to be bridled. When I think back, it would have been those officers who were abusing Judges Rules which caused 'thief catching' to be an activity of the past. No longer would it be used as a measure of a detective's worthiness about how many 'coughs' he could extract from suspects by whatever means.

3. The Tide Turns – A Fresh Start

It was due to this situation of, in most cases, 'tinkering' and in a very small minority of cases, sheer criminality, that PACE was laid on the statute book. Suddenly, suspects were protected by a wide-ranging piece of legislation and a gaggle of custody sergeants and their staff who believed that it was their 'job's worth' not to protect the prisoners in their custody to the nth degree.

No-one could blame them, but my contention is that whoever it was in the Home Office who first sat down to commence the first draft, had too much of a false perception of the problems to be solved. They had a difficult job to do but from what resulted, they clearly had never worked on criminal investigations themselves and had used a massive hammer to crack this nut. The management of arrested suspects could so easily have been tightened without placing so many weights on the suspects' side of the scales of justice so as to cause those investigating them to hold up their hands in despair and exclaim, "Why should we bother"?

Who could have believed that this had caused a sudden lack of interest in the CID which, at one time, was the most sought-after appointments in the job. It was only a few months ago when I was astounded when seeing an advertisement from the West Mercia force, for recruits to be directly entered into the CID. My assumption was that that ludicrous move had been made because of the lack of interest in becoming a detective.

The rules that were being bent were all straightened out but, the burden of trying to detect heinous crimes with time constraints which may involve many suspects, was just one example which caused detectives to go back to fishing or any other hobby other than the professional thief catching that they so much enjoyed. 99% of them were good men and women and they had their hands tied behind their backs to the detriment of victims and the criminal justice system.

Back in 1981, before the implementation of PACE and as a detective superintendent, I had actually experienced the problem with having to arrest four suspects of a murder quite quickly in succession. Two had been arrested soon after the offence but another two suspects had been identified during their interviews. They had to be arrested as quickly as possible because of the dangers involved in leaving them to interfere with witnesses, hone up alibi's or even abscond. But I, with another detective was in the process of interviewing the original suspects and we could not possibly leave them to interview the others. It was therefore necessary to call in two other DCIs to in effect, link with us and to interview these additional two suspects. That was done out of a practical necessity **AND THERE WAS NO CLOCK RUNNING**. It does not require any explanation from me to be able to imagine how difficult it would be with the restrictions of PACE being applied. I have no doubts that with them, those additional two suspects would not have been taken off the streets so early because they would have been in custody with the clock running but would not have been properly interviewed. We have got ourselves into a ludicrous situation now and no-one appears to be shouting about it. 'Why Bother' pertains! The baby had been thrown out with the bath water. Thief catchers had been identified and rose to the surface from their skills in a police uniform. They had demonstrated an aptitude for it which most others did not hold.

It is not only the difficulty of dealing with multiple suspects that raises its head these days. There cannot be too many people in this world who have now not witnessed suspects been interviewed 'real time' on TV. In addition, there cannot be too many suspects who have been seen to answer the police questions put to them, that is, other than saying 'NO COMMENT'. Suspects were always told that they need not say anything in answer to police questioning. That was their human right however, not answering them used to be very much the exception rather than the rule. It was the skill of the investigator that overcame that but now, suspects' lawyers, being paid to do what they should do, will invariably advise their clients to say nothing. This has resulted in suspects now repeated those two words, 'NO COMMENT' to every question even those about non-related matters. "How do you feel today"? – "NO COMMENT"!! Is this justice?

The screening of such cases and their ensuing interviews quickly taught everyone, not only the suspects involved but the thousands of TV watching suspects of the future, that they need not at all, be compelled to answer any questions the police put to them. All they had to say was, "NO COMMENT". I quickly emphasise that nothing else had changed because whilst they were always informed of their rights, they often wanted to convince the investigator of their innocence but now, after watching the 'NO COMMENT' interviews, their stance has changed. The solicitors who were now specialising in representing defendants also caught on possibly even quicker, because making no comments by their clients made their jobs much easier. Apart from their client's not speaking, all they had to do now was to wait until they were served with the file of evidence by the prosecution and then review what was best for their clients.

Some cases might then involve putting their clients hands up to plead guilty but with others, a defendant's trial in court would not only be best for their clients, but getting involved in trials would suit their businesses even better. The bitter pill to swallow, is that these 'fly on the wall' cases which, in my estimation have been so needlessly facilitated by the police to be screened, have caused our criminals to now become so aware of modern forensic methods that they have learned how best to avoid detection. We have already seen that due to mobile phone forensics, criminals are now using other methods to communicate and mostly, this will involve the use of pre-paid 'burner' phones which can be discarded as and when they feel is necessary.

Of course, being their human right with nothing much else changing, has witnessed our criminals now being raised in an era containing a much higher profile of those human rights and at the same time, a lowering of crime detection rates. They have been educated by television, or having been incarcerated in some overcrowded place of detention where prisoners learn from each other. OK, a good thing most would say but suddenly, there was not a lot of point in arresting suspects unless the evidence had previously been obtained that went a long way to proving their guilt. The only motivation left in arresting suspects would involve the obtaining of more forensic evidence from them and their environment. No longer was the skill of interviewing required. A robot might as well do it.

I hope you are ahead of me because, in the example I have described above, not arresting those suspects very early due to the fear of 'the clock' would have left an awful lot to be desired. In addition, our recruits now, have been raised in this same era and they too have been educated within their police training and onward careers. They will know no different and hence will not be attracted to use the skills which some of them may have inherently possessed and may well have been put to good use.

Yes, we could also legally lock suspects up on a Friday and leave them in the cells until Monday and if, often, they had softened up and co-operated, we would charge and bail them accordingly and without reference to anyone other than a supervisor accepting the charges. There were no time constraints and apart from being served a writ of 'habeas corpus', suspects were ours to deal with appropriately. It is impossible for me to allege that all were properly cared for but if not, those cases would be in such a tiny minority as to be of insignificant weight to have this nut needlessly cracked as described previously.

That was at a time that called for better suspect care but what has not been generally stated is that almost without exception, such suspects were known to have definitely committed the offences. Invariably, they will have been 'put in' by mates or paid informants. Or simply that other evidence had been found. They will more than likely have been one of those from families responsible for 80% of the crime on your patch or had left their particular 'Modus Operandi' at the scene.

When as a chief superintendent on secondment to Her Majesty's Inspector of Constabulary's office, (HMIC) I was required to undergo this PACE training because of course, I was one of those later expected to review cases in progress and if appropriate, sign permissions to detain suspects for extended periods. So, having done this job of extending the time constraints myself, I could not understand how on earth they could investigate serious and protracted cases with more than one suspect unless given the additional time. I had already tasted that a few years earlier.

The law now demands that they be charged or released generally within 24 hours or subject to smaller justified extensions if appropriate. I can now understand why they were now forced to leave the arrest to as late a time possible, but of course, as hinted above, that would mean leaving a bad person free to commit other crimes or cover their tracks and sometimes evidence could disappear and that was very dangerous.

It is those 'Fly on the wall' documentaries which identify why it is that arresting suspects without any forensic or technical evidence to support charges, is now almost a futile operation. I wondered how on earth we managed with no CCTV evidence, no mobile phone forensic technology, no automatic number plate recognition, no body worn cameras, no social media, and the host of other forensic digital aids now on show in these programs.

But then, we did not have the time constraints built into PACE and it is only now, in 2023 that I can understand why few want to join the CID and why adverts are appearing for recruits to directly join their CID ranks.

By the time I had been re-employed with West Marcia Police in their 'Retained Experienced Personnel' scheme and ordered to take my two-day Diversity Training in May 2002, this change had all happened in those eight years since my retirement in 1994. I was shell shocked. I could not believe the change and I wrote about it but merely as a passing comment. I had not realised the extent of the changes made but since my first cries of anguish, I have had my eyes opened even more. As mentioned above, I am not against the principles of human rights, diversity or the benefits of health and safety but their hands are being overplayed at the expense of common sense. If that's 'Wokism' then I am against it. We must treat each other fairly but for goodness' sake, let's get on with policing for the benefit of society and of course, the victims who always get forgotten in such matters.

Our new recruits have all now been educated and police trained in what they might describe as a more enlightened society. Remarkably, it is that society which now suggests that it is OK to drag down the statues of those who were our historical heroes. That used to be known as 'Criminal Damage'. The organisation 'PRIDE' became a popular activist lobby and the term LGBT+ was a new term I had to learn to decipher and understand. It is only a few years ago that if you were gay, there was no chance of you joining the police force and if you were in it and discovered, then watch out! Now we have associations for gay people and those in the ethnic minorities. We have evolved, that is fine. We now discover that radical university students with a 'Left Wing' ideology are cancelling out certain lectures carried out by lecturers who do not confirm to their ideologies. **WHAT?** University authorities have stood by whilst colluding in some instances with these stances. A University of Sussex Professor has recently been hounded out of her job by transgender activists. Museums are now removing their exhibits; lecturers are now ignoring previously well-known and respected authors and I now read that free thinking scholars are being drummed out of universities by transgender activists. The Times newspaper reports that it now feels more like a surrender. I just could not believe what was going on……. however –

EUREKA !!

This is an inserted section of this diatribe, the date of which, when I typed it was 18th November 2022, when finally, the penny had dropped. I rose at around 6am after lying in bed tossing and turning over in my mind what it was that turned that tide of change to the degree that I have described above. I had finally woken to the obvious which had been staring me in my face for years. With me believing that I had been a fairly good detective, I am almost ashamed to admit that I had missed it. Yet reading what I had already written above, I had actually been spelling it out – but had not fully reasoned that when all these things were joined up, then that was the final answer: -

THAT RE-SET BUTTON MUST HAVE BEEN PRESSED OVER AND OVER AGAIN MANY TIMES IN THAT EIGHT YEAR PERIOD FROM AROUND THE TIME I HAD RETIRED FROM CARRYING A WARRANT CARD ON 28TH NOVEMBER 1994, TO SOMETIME PREVIOUS TO MAY 2002 WHEN I BECAME RE-EMPLOYED IN WEST MERCIA! I shall later suggest that that period of my re-education, would be during the late 1980s.

Blimey, yes, Yes, Yes, Yes. Of course, members of all forces have suffered wholesale changes of personality and culture and if I describe them as being 'Indoctrinated' I hope I am not over exaggerating and that it will be understood what I mean in the context of the changes I explore. It was just that the police force and all who sailed in her had become a 'new breed'. **WHAT** indeed had happened? Time had moved on so quickly that new generations with new ideas and concepts had arrived and gone. On average, a new generation appears after about 20 years. It has now been 29 years since I retired and that's almost one and a half generations!

I suddenly realised that very senior chief constables were very young when I retired, and they would not have known what the concepts of Local and Residential Beat Officers were all about. They may not have seen a village police station or even a 'Panda Car' so when they speak about a desire to support 'Community Policing', what image do they have in their minds? For example: -

Pippa Mills, the current chief constable of West Mercia joined the police just two years after I retired. Martin Hewitt, chief constable, and the current Chairman of the National Police Chiefs' Council (NPCC) was born in 1966 when I had three years of regular service. (And when England won the World Cup!) He joined Kent Police in 1993, just one year before I retired. Chief Constable Andy Marsh, the director of the 'College for Policing' joined the police in 1987, 27 years after I had joined.

All of these and no doubt all other current chief officers of police had joined the police AFTER or AROUND PACE being implemented and after the Crown Prosecution Service had been implemented and, even after the Human Rights Act 1988 became law. They will all be completely oblivious of 'Life on Mars' during those policing with the consent of the community days.

As an aside, and with reference to both Martin Hewitt and Andy Marsh's present occupations, I learn that small changes had already occurred in the titles of the agencies they represent as follows: -

The National Police Chiefs' Council (NPCC) has been changed from what used to be 'The Association of Chief Police Officers'. (ACPO) The College of Policing has been changed from 'The Police College'. In both cases, I ask myself, "WHY"?

Yes, evolution in the context of its own definition does mean change; but surely it implies changes for the better, or at least, are reasonable and to a justifiable degree, sufficient to cure the ills required to be cured?

I became fully employed abroad and this had taken me away from my contacts and detailed knowledge of what was going on in the police service of England and Wales. I found the need to research this era and so what I write here, is merely what I discovered since that EUREKA moment and would not have been in my mind at the time because I knew nothing about it. Whatever the merits of the arguments on either side, this situation ended with the passing of 'The Human Rights Act 1998'. I had learned that this legislation was based on articles of the European Convention of Human Rights. Without mentioning the minutia of every provision, it facilitated and emphasised many human rights which had been so deep-rooted previously that they were regarded already to be rights automatically to be applied. So, in drafting this legislation, an emphasis was placed towards those accused of wrongdoing and who may therefore, end up accused in the courts.

This new legislation compelled public organisations, including the government, police and local councils to treat everyone with fairness, dignity and respect. It also emphasised the prohibition of torture and inhuman treatment, protection against slavery and forced labour and the right to liberty and freedom and many other similar concepts. Similarly, the right for free speech and peaceful protest to express views was encapsulated along with everyone's right being equal. People should not be treated unfairly because of, for example, gender, race, disability, sexuality, religion or age. Again, I emphasise that the description above is only in part, the main emphasis of the legislation.

I conclude that the provisions mentioned above were already in place and that the police, were operating that way since they took the oath. But I could not help questioning myself. Was I so naïve that this measure had become necessary?

My work with fingerprint systems abroad and later, back in the UK concluded in 2002 and among other engagements, I became the manager of a senior school where I was responsible for everything other than teaching. Those responsibilities included all 'Health and Safety' issues and embraced a great deal of diversity and inclusive practices. The Equality Act 2010 which legally protected people from discrimination in the workplace and in wider society replaced previous anti-discrimination laws with a single Act and I can only surmise that with the above 'Human Right's legislation, this had triggered our police service into ensuring in their own ways, that they had to be seen as being fully compliant.

So, where are the human rights and equality of the victim, which in my view, should be framed so as to insist that anyone suspected of committing such a crime, should be expected to answer any reasonable questions put to them by the investigators? The fact that unless torture is applied, no suspect can be physically compelled to say anything might have something to do with it. However, no adverse comment can be made to the jury by those prosecuting or by the judge about the defendant not answering questions unless special circumstances exist. It is a travesty of justice in my opinion even though I fully realise such comment has been made before but I believe it is worth repeating here. Is not that plain common sense and fair? Apparently not!

Watching the true crime 'cold cases' on television serves to understand that unless there is good additional, (more than likely) forensic evidence to rely upon, then suspect perpetrators will not be charged. The scales of justice have been weighing very heavily on the sides of suspects for far too long. I think on reflection, that I may have been a part of the start of such changes but had not then realised it. To explain in more detail, there is a requirement for me to set the scene when this began by returning much earlier to the so called 'Good Old Days' which you might have realised by now, were not that good anyway.

You may not initially, draw connections with 1976 but please bear with me, as I need to start from my earlier policing days as follows. On 29th March 1976 I was suddenly promoted to chief inspector and to take up the position of 'Deputy Commandant' of our force's training school. In that capacity, I had supervised an intake of a cadet course of about fifty or so cadets. All young boys and a scattering of girls who were to spend 12 months at the school much like a boarding school. The personalities of them as a group, and the training and discipline they received at the school, plays a very important part in identifying how and when the transformation of the culture of the police service would have commenced. Yes, I am trying to remember when it was that such social and cultural changes were made in the police service?

I was the discipline authority and although I had not any prior experience in the 'police training' world, I got on well with these cadets and of course, the more senior of constables and officers of higher rank attending other courses. So, this has been a long-winded way of explaining that I and other members of staff at the school can certify that those cadets we worked with in that 1977 era were trained in the same fashion as we had been. For better or for worse, they were shouted at, disciplined and trained in that 'old school' talk and chalk manner and encouraged to question what was taught.

Many of us have kept in touch with them and have even attended their reunions after they, themselves had retired. There was never any sign of changes in training methods and definitely, 'Wokism' or whatever is meant by that term, was never on the horizon. The same applied at the time of my retirement in 1994.

Also, if you recall what I said previously, it was in May 2002 when I had been so surprised in having to attend a Diversity Course at Kidderminster when I re-joined as a member of the 'Retained Experienced Personnel' Scheme. This was of course, after the new Human Rights legislation but prior to the 'Equality Act' of 2010. We can therefore narrow down when it was that 'important' changes in training methods and the effects of 'Wokism' began to slowly surface and have a consequence. It would be during that eight-year period from 1994 to 2002.

Those cadets were more than likely to have been one of the last 'Old School'. They were an 'Intake' that managed to retire without witnessing any vast changes that had appeared in that era. Our Chief Constable, Alex Rennie would not have had a whiff of what was to come. Indeed, when he retired in 1981, we were still very much in the 'Old School'. Many will remember him featuring in cartoon fashion on the front cover of the national 'Police' magazine. He was depicted as the chief with extra-large boots with which he could tread all over those beneath him. This was a characterisation drawn by DC John Edwards of our force who became a popular and very good 'police' cartoonist as well as a good detective constable, he was a gentleman and a friend of mine.

Alex was far removed from being a 'modern day' chief and was renowned for being somewhat of a bully and a harsh disciplinarian but many of us half held our hands up for him at least being a chief who spoke his mind and was not afraid to upset the Home Office or anyone else. However, he of that ilk had to change with the times, and yes, it must be conceded that he would not have survived as a chief for very long after he eventually retired. It was in his retirement that he wrote a book of his life story. It is entitled, 'Farm Hand to Chief Constable'. So, it is only because one can gauge the type of chief constable he was, I reproduce in its entirety, that written on the rear cover of it here and to emphasise that chief constables with his background, would not become chief constables in our changed era of today: -

> On leaving school at 14, Alex Rennie worked as a second horseman at Nether Mill Farm in Birness, Aberdeenshire during the depression years of the early 1930s. Studying in the evenings after a hard day in the fields paid rewards when he joined the Durham County Constabulary in 1937.
>
> On the outbreak of war, Alex trained in sabotage to counter the feared German invasion. When that threat diminished, despite being in a reserve occupation, Alex applied to join the armed services. Refusing to accept 'no' for an answer, Alex applied every month until the powers that be relented. Being personally briefed for a secret assignment by Winston Churchill, Alex qualified as a pilot at West Point before being commissioned in the Royal Northumberland Fusiliers for active service in Europe.
>
> Back in the Police Force, Alex never saw himself as a high-flyer, conscientiously performing, and enjoying, his role as 'Bobby on the Beat' for eleven years before starting his inexorable rise to the higher echelons of policing, ending up as Chief Constable of West Mercia.

Alex's strong work ethic and his firm but fair common-sense approach shine through every page of this eminently readable book.

The world needs more like Alex Rennie!

It is the final sentence which if written more recently, would unfortunately cause most readers to gulp, for it nicely portrays that Alex was one of the last of the 'Old School'. Maybe the world requires leaders with more pluck and emphasis of that ilk but not chief constables. Alex died on 8th July 2011 but following his 1981 retirement, I served under a gaggle of other chief constables for the ensuing years of my service and later as a member of the 'REP' scheme.

Thankfully, they were all of a completely different disposition to one another, but some paid more attention to being nice and liked than being concerned with commanding. David Blakey who unfortunately has become unwell recently stands out as one of the better ones, probably the best of the bunch. He went on to be a regional HMI and like Alex, he too, had arrived from Durham.

It was in January 1985 when, resulting from being in the right place at the right time, I received another very surprising promotion to chief superintendent and became a staff officer to HMI Mr. John Woodcock who had inspected my Bromsgrove Sub Division prior to selecting me.

I shall not name him but from the sequence of events, those who want to discover who it was will calculate it. Here was a completely different character to Alex Rennie. Suddenly those who wanted to grow beards were allowed to and our lady spouses and partners had formed a weekly coffee morning in the police clubs of various police stations. He was loved by all.

Suddenly, this new breed of chief constables was among us, not that we had not realised that evolution had started to turn the tide. There remained a few of the type I have described in the likes of Alex Rennie but I guess on reflection, this was the period when we were changing the characters and philosophies of our chief officers. I recall the Chief Constable of the Greater Manchester Police, Sir James Anderton who led that force for sixteen years from 1975 to 1991 and without doubt, possessed one of the highest profiles and the respect of our police chiefs of that era. I never saw Sir James in the flesh and obviously never spoke to him but his period in office encompassed the period when I worked at the police inspectorate, and I can confirm that his dogged voice and command of policing matters became a thorn in the flesh of the Home Office. He commanded with a persona, presence and a voice heard loud and clear which was often, heard by all those having an interest in policing. My position in the Inspectorate afforded me glimpses into that being circulated among the five regional HMI's offices and with the Home Office. I enjoyed reading what he was up to.

He, like Alex Rennie, needed to command and that would have been a difficult task by some of those who followed their retirements. Many liked them because they stood and acted for what they believed. The refusal by Alex to allow officers to grow beards is a good example. He thought that growing them was being lazy and not conducive to smartness. I am not suggesting that his thoughts were correct, but I am suggesting that that sort of brittle front leadership and sense of commanding is now missing. Neither he, nor Sir James would have had the time or inclination to even discuss the changing of their minds on such issues or even starting coffee clubs for our ladies.

It is not that I would have ever objected to such happenings, it was just that those 'Old School' leaders would not have put them so high in their order of priorities, if at all. Finding such characters in the police service as Alex and Sir James today, is an impossibility because such species simply do not exist anymore, so far as I am aware. No one shouts about their perceived injustices in the police service anymore. We are missing such firm commanders who, to put it bluntly, would not pussy foot around watching extremists pull down statues and block motorways.

John Woodcock told me many years later after we had both retired, how our new Chief had 'pussy footed' about my promotion and was in his opinion, afraid, and perhaps reluctant to return to the force, faced with having to promote someone (me) ahead of the queue. Alex Rennie would have had no fears if he thought the right person had got the job.

My other memory of Alex was on an occasion when caught in the right mood probably in his retirement, I told him that despite his reputation, he couldn't have been that bad because he had promoted me several times. He snarled and in his broad Scottish accent retorted, "We can all make mistakes Humph"! Thinking about this, we must have both been in our retirements otherwise, I would have been a contender for being posted to the furthest point north!

I have recalled these incidents merely to differentiate between the breed of Chief Constables since that **'Eureka'** moment hit me, many pages ago. How on earth had I missed this 'RE-SET' of the whole nature and culture of every police force and their chief officers?

Those cadets that I hopefully had proudly influenced back in 1976/7 had now all retired. I still know many of them in their own retirements today. I had not realised what had happened when on a later occasion, an old solicitor friend of mine asked me for good reason, if I could, as a particular favour, contact any of the chief officers in West Mercia. I can recall telling him that by now, there would not be one serving officer in West Mercia who would have been in the job at the same time as myself. They were all now either 'passed on' or had retired! That was the truth and the realisation of it then hit me. How quickly does time fly and how quickly does fashion and changes travel with it.

Even by 2002, not many police officers in West Mercia had been so experienced in operating computers and that was the main reason why I had been asked to return and examine crime patterns and the methods of working with computers, particularly the recording of them and the subsequent progress of the investigations. I was also used as a software trainer in other aspects of policing.

So, apart from this work I became involved in, I had not explored to any great depth, the reasons why those changes had occurred and what affects they had on the policing of the community. I had not then met or had been introduced to the new generation of policing in the era of what very loosely is now described as 'Wokism'. I now confess that I had trod far too softly when describing those changes in my last book, but it had been those drastic recent criticisms which make me hopefully, hit a little harder here.

It was just another tragedy which, on this same date that I had typed that 'EUREKA' heading that, yet another 'Police Cock Up' was to hit our media with the inevitable accompanying flood of criticism as depicted in the headlines below.

Criticism of the Police had now become an almost daily feature in the 'popular tabloid' press and indeed, also in the more 'highbrow' media. I have always been something of a 'social' animal and a member of various public service and sports clubs where my colleagues in them, were also not holding back from asking questions about police failures of the type I was having difficulty in defending. The family of a mother and daughter murdered by the daughter's abusive ex-partner in 2018 say they were failed 'beyond imagination' after a coroner ruled police errors contributed to their deaths.

Raneem Oudeh, 22, was murdered outside her mother Khowla Saleem's home in Solihull, West Midlands, just after midnight on August 27, 2018. The pair were violently stabbed to death by Janbaz Tarin as Ms Oudeh was on the phone to police at the time. Tarin, who admitted the killings, was jailed for life with a minimum of 32 years in December 2018. This media outburst was as a result of the Coroner's Inquest. In a damning judgement, the coroner concluded that deaths were materially contributed to by the failings of the West Midlands Police. This brought the usual apology with 'Lessons will be learned' speech by the force's Assistant Chief Constable Andy Hill.

After being begged to respond on the telephone in an emergency call, the estranged husband of the daughter, was at the same time stabbing his victims to death. The Police failed to turn up because "they were busy at a firearms incident". In a statement, Mr Hill said: **"On behalf of West Midlands Police, I would like to apologise to Raneem and Khaola's family – we should have done more. Their dignity throughout the inquest has been humbling. More could have been done to protect Raneem from the campaign of domestic abuse that she suffered in the months leading up to her death at the hands of the man who would go on to kill her and her mother".**

Mail Online

Home | NEWS | U.S. | Sport | TV&Showbiz | Australia | Femail | Health | Science | Money |

'We're sorry - we could have saved them': Police apologise to young mother, 22, and her mother murdered by her estranged husband after she made FOUR 999 calls begging for help

- Janbaz Tarin, 25, murdered wife Raneem Oudeh and her mother Khaola Saleem
- Ms Oudeh had desperately called 999 four times on the night of her murder
- But she and her mother were stabbed to death while she was speaking to police
- An inquest has found errors by West Midlands Police contributed to the tragedy

Published on 18ᵗʰ November 2022 by Mail Online

"The events leading up to this awful tragedy have rightly been examined in detail in the inquest and by other organisations to ensure that lessons can be learned and to give the families the answers they deserve". He continued, "It is clear that we should have done more to join-up the incidents of abuse that were being reported to us so that the officers considering Raneem's case had a full picture of the ordeal that Raneem was enduring at the hands of Janbaz Tarin". He continued - "The seriousness and pattern of abuse should have been better recognised, the risk posed by Mr Tarin should have been better assessed and the crimes that were being committed should have been better identified and investigated, with action taken against Mr Tarin".

Oh, come on – how pathetic that statement must be and how pathetic is the Police Service seen in such lights? We have already learned the lessons time and time again. What is needed is a complete overall and, in some cases, a reversal to the way emergency calls had been handled in the past. If that means replacing civilian clerks or inexperienced officers with experienced police officers, then so be it!

I am now hesitantly turning the pages of newspapers hoping and praying no more examples of police ineffectiveness are among them. Things were not always brilliant in my day, and I can even disclose that despite my criticisms here, I am being slightly hypocritical because all of us in the 'police family' will know that such tragedies can easily happen again. But things have so obviously got very much worse and there must be an underlying reason or probably many of them, why that is so.

Is it a coincidence that complaints against police failing to arrive at reports of crime or who have arrived at them at much slower speeds, have increased by 11% compared with last year. These figures have been published by the Independent Office for Police Conduct (IOPC). They received 75,020 such complaints in England and Wales in the year to 31st March 2022. Forces took an average of nine working days to contact a complainant. **WHAT?** We would have been reprimanded had we not contacted a complainant on the same day and before our shift concluded.

And so, we have arrived at our 'New School' era to find that it is not just the police in this hot water. The NHS with their hospital beds not available causing patients to wait inexcusable lengths of time in ambulances, and with the courts with the longest backlog of cases ever and our prisons full, we seem to be sinking deeper and deeper into a state of being incapable of managing our growing population and its requirements.

4. The 'New School'.

It was during the period of my retirement whilst working with the 'Retained Experienced Personnel' scheme, that by chance, the new Chief Constable, Paul West was being shown around the headquarters at Hindlip Hall, and as I worked alone at a desk in the Criminal Intelligence section, and was obviously retired, I was introduced to him so that I could explain what our 'REP' scheme was all about. After all, there was only a handful of us old dogs employed as such. Mr West had been appointed chief in August 2003 and so this would have been soon after I had re-commenced working there.

By now, the number of chief constables heading the West Mercia Constabulary was rapidly increasing. Of the names I can recall since retirement would be Bob Cozens, Tony Mullett, David Blakey and Peter Hampson. Tony Mullett and David Blakey had served in the Association of Chief Officer (ACPO) ranks at other forces and with us in West Mercia before becoming our chief constables. I am pretty sure however, that neither Tony Mullett or his successor, David Blakey had a great deal to do with the changes incorporating this 'New Generation' of Police Officers. After all, I was still serving but that did not guarantee that I knew exactly what was going on at our police training centres, in the halls of Westminster or at the Home Office when such far-reaching changes were being contemplated.

But hang on! When I worked with the HMIC, we were just one of five regional offices and in the words of my boss, Sir John Woodcock, we were employed "Of the police force but not in it and in the Home Office but not of it". Although I had been promoted as a police chief superintendent, I had been informed that I was now a civil servant working at the Home Office. It seemed very strange. Each of the five HMIC offices were similarly staffed with two secretaries, two chief superintendent staff officers a chief inspector 'Clerk / Administrator' and a driver. The two staff officers were seconded for two years and in order that one could learn from the other, whenever one of our secondments concluded, we rotated the forces so that the new incumbent took over the same forces which the remaining staff officer had been responsible for in their first year. In addition, to carrying out pre-inspections in those forces, we also looked after their interests with anything going on with them from a Home Office point of view. For example, I recall visiting the G3 Division at the main Home Office building at Queen Ann's Gate in connection with the building of a new force headquarters for Leicestershire, which finally came to fruition.

The system worked very well and enabled me to learn so much more about the work of those civil servants and the administration within the Home Office which of course, was where the Chief HMI's office was located. These were the days prior to computer literacy spreading its wings, especially throughout the police service. Our secretaries used word processors but that would have been about the limit of their computer software skills.

We were, however blessed with a chief inspector who was years ahead of us in that respect. Chris Gray had been seconded from the West Midlands Police and memory tells me that he was a graduate. He was very bright and also very able to use his personal computer to produce all kinds of spreadsheets and tables. I know that following his secondment, he quickly shot up the ladder and was himself, a chief superintendent in his own force, and though my memory fades, I am pretty sure he ended up as a Chief Officer in another force after I had retired from the service.

My job involved analysing the performance of my forces and part of this involved comparing them with other 'like' forces. I quickly became familiar with the 'Chartered Institute of Public Finance and Accountancy' (CIPFA) statistics. I was able to discover a huge range of statistical data comparisons for all forces in every aspect of their policing. As an unusual and extreme example, due to our interest being drawn to the poor conditions of one force fleet of vehicles, I recall that they were able to tell me the average number of miles their police vehicles had travelled before they were replaced. They did indeed, indicate that the force in question should renew their vehicles far sooner than they had been doing. The system worked and the mechanics were delighted.

The statistics in themselves were obviously very boring but they represented base material from which could be explored further in the performance of

'Pre-Inspections' and when eventually compiling my HMI's brief for the forces' annual inspections proper.

I chatted to Chris and in no time at all, he produced what I now know as Excel spreadsheets comprising comparisons in any form desired – 'Pye' and 'Bar' charts etc and in a variety of colours to boot. We showed this to the HMI and he was like a dog with two tails. When scrutinising our reports, we learned that The Home Office loved them too and before we knew where we were, we had christened them 'Performance Indicators' which the Home Office wanted all other HMIs to produce and use. From then on, the results of the comparison were always subject to our discussions with the chief constables on the first day of each force inspection. Each inspection ended on the last day with a lunch with the Police Authorities and you could bet that they were also raised there by the HMI in his after-lunch talk to them.

I was not to know that together, Chris and I had produced the ammunition which often caused damning wounds to our leaders in the police and although I always worked to ensure that so far as possible, the divisions in which I subsequently worked, performed efficiently so as to be shielded from such wounds, these performance indicators quickly transformed into 'Working by Objectives' an animal which, as a Divisional Commander, had often tied me to my desk for longer than I always thought necessary. Perhaps in a strange way, I was partially to blame for all this desk work. I had shot myself in the foot. I had always wanted to be doing the job and not stuck in my office writing about how well we had done and how we were going to keep to that standard in the future.

So, my view was that the police service had 'knee jerked' itself into a giant over reaction which caused such measures such as 'five-year plans' being demanded by the 'top landing'. What had we done? Forces were appointing small 'in force' inspection teams whose job it was, concerned the assurance that us Divisional Commanders were going to keep the forces' heads above the water and thus free from criticism. Inevitably, our 'five year' plans would need reviewing annually and in simple terms, a new fifth year plan would replace the first-year plan which had now expired. In reality, most items in any policing plan would need to rely on finance which appeared never to be available. So, despite most plans never coming to fruition, we needed to waste more time (in my estimation) by replacing them with more plans which were expected to experience similar fates.

Since those 'HMI' days, I experienced being a Divisional Commander of two Divisions (Redditch and the Traffic and Operations Division) and latterly, having shed the 'Traffic' element, the head of the 'Operations' Department. I found myself writing more and more 'gobbledegook' and although I cannot completely blame myself and Chris Gray for being responsible, there had always been a seed of doubt about whether those early 'Performance Indicators' had grown beyond recognition into a small element which eventually caused me a little pleasure in handing in my notice of retirement. It was only in hindsight that I can now see that we were beginning to lose our way.

I now believe that we are suffering today, from another 'knee jerk' and overzealous blast of reactions to the 'Human Rights' and 'Equality' issues and processes launched in the recent past. The subjects are different, but their ethos is similarly being reacted to and felt. Are we throwing the baby out with the bathwater?

Both issues embroiled with human rights and equality are extremely important and although I believe in the merits of the legislation surrounding them, I ask if we have once again taken our eyes off the ball and not on the activities contained in both the old and new versions of the oath, which in any event, includes respecting human rights and equality.

I was surprised to see the changes contained in the Police Act 1996 which also included changes made to the oath I took, when upon being attested into the office of constable. Here it is as it was back then in 1960: -

> *I, do solemnly, sincerely and truly declare and affirm that I will faithfully discharge the duties of the office of constable with fairness, integrity, diligence and impartiality, and that I will uphold fundamental human rights and accord equal respect to all people, according to law.*

So, fairness and human rights were, after all included back then! I now discover that although the theme running through it is very similar, that the oath has, by virtue of the Police Act 1996 changed as follows: -

I (name) ...of (police force)... do solemnly and sincerely declare and affirm that I will well and truly serve the King in the office of constable, with fairness, integrity, diligence and impartiality, upholding fundamental human rights and according equal respect to all people; and that I will, to the best of my power, cause the peace to be kept and preserved and prevent all offences against people and property; and that while I continue to hold the said office I will to the best of my skill and knowledge discharge all the duties thereof faithfully according to law.

I am having difficulty in spotting the differences. Surely It is fundamentally the same?

So, returning to that era of change, David Blakey was our Chief between 1991 and 1999 when he became an HMI. The PACE Act 1984 had already been implemented, as did the changes made due to the implementation of the Crown Prosecution Service. Brain was very clearly preferred to the 'Brawn' of the past and Mr Blakey had been wise enough to study for an MBA with the Open University, I believe when he had been an inspector in the Durham force prior to him joining us as our Assistant Chief Constable. We had both joined the force as cadets in 1960 but he being much wiser, preferred to earn his degree whilst I was probably wasting my time playing some sport or other.

The desire to have degree holders as senior officers was, in my estimation, 'on track' and indeed, that was one of the elements in my decision not to seek advancement into the 'Chief Officer ranks'. Of course, I had not got a GCE let alone a degree and having failed with one application to join the Senior Command course, after Tony Mullett had advised me that things might have been different had I possessed a degree, I told him that I would not be making any further applications.

Let me say at the outset that since being introduced to Paul West, a string of coincidences and a touch of fate was to be responsible for the development of quite a close relationship between us.

On that day when we first met, he immediately struck me as a completely different 'animal' (Just a term Paul!) to those Chief Officers I had once worked with when operating as John Woodcock's staff officer. Of course, I had met many of them in that role and was trusted to the extent that I was never far away from his side even when they spoke in confidence. At well over six feet tall, with good looks thrown in, Paul West's physical appearance in uniform was enviable. He had been blessed with the right tools and I rightly or wrongly saw him as among one of the first of our new breed of Chief Officers.

In 2004, I wrote to Paul to ask him if he would accept becoming the 'Honourary Member' of our Rotary Club of which I was then the president. He accepted the invitation and by the way, he undoubtedly attended more meetings and functions as such than any other honourary member I can recall in my experience as a Rotarian. He was most definitely of that modern day mould and was miles away from the likes of Alex Rennie. That old mould had been cast aside and a new one had been forged. I would not have been concerned about him being judged for his operational prowess and although I did not then know anything about his operational past, he did not strike me as being a 'thief catcher' but if not, he obviously fitted the desired mould of the day, by use of his skills in management as opposed to much else. He had attained more than one academic degree and played the violin to a very high standard. He was surely representing the 'New Generation' of policing, or at least that of police chiefs.

I have had the pleasure of publicly thanking Paul on more than one occasion when he had volunteered to speak after dinner on various issues. I could carry on about his qualities, but the object of this section is to identify the stark contrast between the 'Old School' chiefs and our modern-day equivalent.

But I cannot leave this 'Paul West' section without reference to an amusing story about him. The head of year eleven at the challenging senior school where I last worked asked me if I could get someone of 'dignitary' status who would be prepared to present some prizes to her year eleven students. She was one of the few good teachers I worked with and wanted to encourage those in her year who were struggling. She came up with the idea that at her next year's assembly, she would provide gifts for the most 'improved' students in various subjects, as opposed to the normal 'best' students.

Paul West never hesitated and there he was on the due day as smart as I knew he would be in his uniform. I had the list of prize winners, and it was my job to announce the subject and to hand Paul the prize so he could present it and shake the winning student's hand. After many prizes had been presented, I duly announced, "This prize is for the **'most improved attendance record'** and with that, I announced the winner to come forward. We were then met with a cacophony of voices, **"He's not in today Sir"**! We could not stop ourselves from chuckling.

In my view, 'Wokery' is whatever one imagines it to be but I use it very loosely to embroil those overzealous reactions to ideologies such as equality, diversity, inclusiveness, human rights, misogyny, health and safety and the like which, although maybe deemed intrinsic in our police family, does not actually aid the capture of criminals and the preservation of peace.

In so far as senior police appointments are concerned, my only problem with this current era of 'Wokery' is that the switch must surely have been pulled too fast and too furiously. It seems to me that we are paying more attention to our cultural ways, means and manners than preventing crime and locking up criminals. My perceptions are based on my own experiences, the volume of critical voice I receive and the content of those objectives, policies, statements or whatever else springs from police headquarters or from the mouths of senior officers in the media, many of whom, find it necessary to read off pre-prepared scripts which doesn't actually fill any audience with confidence. It is also some things that they say which makes me cringe. Only a few days ago, I was listening to my car radio when an assistant chief constable (ACC) was making a statement about the enquiries her force were working on in connection with a brutal shooting to death of a lady. I could tell from how she was delivering her little speech that she was reading it. Anyone who has spoken publicly will have known. She also described the officers working on the case with - **"Me and my team"….** It was only the smallest possible term, but it gave me, and hence others, the impression that she was trying to promote herself when many listeners and all those in the police family will know that she would not have owned that team at all. It is likely that she hadn't performed any duty actually within that investigation and had probably briefed herself sufficiently enough to have put together that weak statement which again, wouldn't have instilled confidence just because of that slip. My assumption of course, but I would bet my life on it. (The fact that the above ACC was a female is neither here nor there but purely coincidental; I've witnessed that phrase used by both genders)

We most definitely deserved a better educated 'top landing' in our police headquarters but all those things I have listed previously under the umbrella of 'Wokism' were now being affected by them. The list of female chief constables rapidly grew from day to day and the hunt was also on for 'Black' chief officers. Of course, many would deserve such elevation but as touched upon earlier, I cannot be dissuaded even if terms such as 'Positive Action Programmes' are used, from believing that in many instances such programmes involved 'Reverse Discrimination', especially in those early days. I bitterly oppose that notion as to apply it, is surely to discriminate against those who deserved the job before those who were actually appointed? (In January 2004, Michael Fuller was appointed Chief of Kent, the first ethnic minority ((black)) Chief Constable and to the time of writing, is the only one.)

It now appears that the police service will almost be insisting on graduate entry recruits or those who agree to study for a degree once they join as apprentices. That 'Microcosm of Society' spread of recruits will sadly no longer apply and the police service will undoubtedly lose those who may have contributed their own life skills at places other than universities. Yes, we need graduates, but we also need those worker bees I have referred to with bags of common sense and experiences of life in other than a privileged / university society.

Surely there remains a requirement that police officers should be able to communicate with all the different social classes; many I knew could swear with the best of the labourers and bricklayers and in the next minute, hold his or her own with a bank manager. If we are now letting loose a whole bunch of graduates to do our policing, then heaven help us. They will be learning their trade without getting to grips with society or deriving the benefit of chatting to the community as they did when village and resident beat bobbies whilst leaning on their bikes or the garden gates of those to whom they chatted. I will dwell more about recruitment and the additional changes made in training methods in a much later chapter but with now having laid down the platforms generally on which new ideologies have been built, I ask, "where has all this led us nowadays"?

In answering that question, I have used my experiences again and this time, I have hopefully delved a lot deeper in trying to understand why and how the changes I had previously written about, have come to join forces in producing what I now fear is a far poorer police service. **THE TIME TO PRESS THAT 'RE-SET' BUTTON HAS ARRIVED AGAIN.** But this time, for the better. But is it too late?

5. The New Artillery

Having taken a 'peek' at the recruitment section of West Mercia Police's website, I can see that both barrels have been loaded for the attack on the old ideologies which apparently require such a whipping into shape so as to introduce the new ones.

As mentioned in my introduction, I had been shocked at the continuing and mounting amount of criticism being aimed at the police and so, this was the first time, I had visited the web sites of my local West Mercia Police and its Police and Crime Commissioner.

Believing that the objectives and policies it contained should be directed at the public to in effect, 'show off' what it was about, I became concerned that the style of writing was clearly not so much about the objectives concerned with policing but more to do with the 'Human Resource' issues of its employees and how they were recruited and went about their duties. It didn't convince me that it was intended to educate members of the public and was more to do with justifying 'wokism' practices and issues. I feel that most people would want to know what they have done and how they had gone about doing it and with what successes had been achieved in their 'policing' pursuits. The 'Human Resources' methods of who they recruit into their workforce is surely the business of the forces themselves; surely the communities they police are content with who they have recruited and under **normal circumstances** will have accepted that their police forces will already have the 'wherewithal' and be professional enough to recruit the right people. I have emboldened the words 'normal circumstances' above in the light of recent controversy in the identification of two police officers, Carrick and Couzens who have both committed the most horrendous of crimes against women. It may well be pertinent in future annual reports publicised, to include how the recruiting processes have been reviewed and hopefully, improved. But otherwise, such matters would not normally fall within published police objectives. So, whilst agreeing with the ideologies of those subjects which unfortunately have now been tagged as 'Wokism' I again declare that I am not overjoyed at them being unnecessarily overplayed.

Having learned that the College of Policing had circulated a Code of Ethics made in 2014, I checked with just a few neighbouring forces and could see that although such statements, objectives and other policies made by forces were similar, they varied in style quite markedly. I should state from the outset that only because I had been a member of the West Mercia Constabulary (now West Mercia Police) I have used their site as my benchmark. It would have been impossible or impracticable to have examined those of each of the forty-three forces in England and Wales. It is for that reason that the inevitable criticism I make will not be about the West Mercia Police nor those who have contributed to the style, but it will be of 'the system' used as an ingredient to produce them. Unfortunately, I was not happy with their style or their unnecessary use if the public weren't going to read or understand them.

I have used the term 'gobbledegook' before in this book but I do not mean it to be disrespectful to anyone (*it does not attract that red line beneath it*) but I can only come up with this term which I concede does sound disrespectable but I do believe it correctly conveys that what it refers to, is unnecessary and often containing platitudes (buzz words) involving most all of those modern adjectives and phrases such as sustainability, inclusiveness, legitimacy, embedded, underpinning, joined up, outcomes, transparency, engagement, reaching out, holistic, even diverseness or divisiveness etc. etc., all of which are now just fashionable buzz words and were not so popular in the past, but more importantly will most likely annoy or irritate the majority of us being policed.

With that in mind, perhaps some are intended as assurances to the Police and Crime Commissioner whose responsibility it is to ensure that the force provides an efficient and effective policing service. That would actually fit as it would if it was intended that the Home Office received it. Obviously, it must surely also be aimed at the police and support staff as it is they who must join in this contract.

Regrettably, it seems that the police service of today believe that they have to appease far more than the communities in which they serve, probably as much or even more so, than those comprising the communities themselves. I believe that members of our communities will be more concerned with the increased costs of policing on their council tax bills and with the parking of cars on the roads outside their windows and with dogs leaving their excrement near to their homes. More so, they do not want their homes invaded by burglars and so would desire that their local police respond to their calls and catch the criminals that do.

Many more are not happy at all with being booked for exceeding the speed limits by very small amounts or of overstaying their times in car parks even if it might not be the police who operate such functions. If I am not mistaken by the signals I am receiving, such matters are only serving to drive what was a thin edge of the wedge between the police and our communities but is now wedged deeper into that gap.

As examples of the style, I refer to, I had used West Mercia's three opening introductory passages of their **'EQUALITY AND INCUSION STRATEGY 2021-2025',** plus the **'Policing Charter'** but being concerned at the length, and that it might be regarded as being disrespectful to the makers, I would just urge readers to read the few documents themselves at: -

https://www.westmercia.police.uk/SysSiteAssets/media/downloads/west-mercia/about-us/diversity-equality-and-inclusion-strategy.pdf

I will just include the 'Foreword' and the document's 'Introduction' here to give a flavour of what I mean. I see that the author of the document is probably a member of the support staff with the title of **'Strategic Equality and Diversity Officer'** and the foreword is also possibly written by another support staff member referred to as an **'Assistant Chief Officer – Director of Business Services'.**

They both will be paid handsomely to do their jobs and I suspect with previous 'Human Resources' experience and according to their job descriptions, they will perform what is asked of them, very well. Their very employment only emphasises the importance attributed to their skills over the normal policing function. If nothing else, I just wish it could be in plainer English rather than what appears these days to be in the necessary gobbledegook.

Here is that Foreword: -

As Chief Officers, here in West Mercia, we are working with our leadership teams at all levels across our organisation to make our service as inclusive, responsive and effective as possible with the aim of delivering excellence in policing to all our diverse communities. Everyone, regardless of their rank or grade or of any aspect of their personal identity has both rights and responsibilities when it comes to bringing diversity, equality and inclusion to life in the workplace and in wider society.

We police by consent, and it is only by understanding and engaging with our diverse communities, inviting their scrutiny and involvement, that we build trust and good relations and can therefore claim policing legitimacy. Our Local Policing Charter outlines our ongoing commitment to improving our local policing in partnership with communities. Engagement with our talented workforce is just as important, ensuring we establish a fair, flexible and inclusive culture which fosters well-being and which allows us to attract and retain a truly diverse pool of officers and staff. These aspirations are set out in our People Strategy, which is driven by our force vision, values and priorities. In this Diversity, Equality and Inclusion strategy, therefore, we set out our commitment and plans for looking critically at all that we do, through the transformative lens of inclusion to deliver a high-quality service that puts people first and protects communities from harm in alignment with our three force priorities: safer people; safer homes and safer roads.

We would like to thank the members of our Staff Support Networks and our Independent Advisory Groups, along with our many partners, including the Police and Crime Commissioner whose Safer West Mercia Plan sets out policing priorities and whose role encompasses governance of this strategy, for all the work they have done directly or indirectly to inform this strategy and its underpinning delivery plans. We will continue to work in partnership with them to monitor our progress against these and invite peer support and scrutiny from our regional and national policing colleagues.

Yes, who am I to know, but as far as I can see, the grammar is perfect but with all those 'flavour of the year' words, does it help to clarify the message or make it easier to be understood? The document is then signed off in the name of the Assistant Chief Officer, Director of Business Services.

Here is the Introduction: -

The legal and national strategic context for our strategy West Mercia Police is committed to playing its part in delivering the Diversity, Equality and Inclusion (DEI) Strategy of the National Police Chief Council (NPCC).

Chief Constables came together through the NPCC committee individually and as a collective in 2018 to set out their pledge for leading on embedding diversity, equality and inclusion in policing. Organisational leadership on diversity and inclusion at all levels in our organisation is vital but it is the responsibility of each individual and each team to ensure they take personal responsibility for bringing this to life.

The strategy outlines three key elements or aspects for our focus, thus providing a broad framework for our DEI policy here in West Mercia: -

- **Our organisation**
- **Our communities**
- **Our partners**

What factors have informed our Strategy and equality objectives?

For each of these areas, our starting point has been to assess where our current performance and outcomes in terms of diversity, equality and inclusion against where we want and need to be. The NPCC self-assessment tool, along with ongoing engagement with staff, officers, communities and partners is an essential part of this benchmarking and of informing our end delivery plans.

Additional tools and resources we use:

• The Duties set out in the Equality Act 2010 and the Human Rights Act 1998.
• NPCC DEI Strategy and toolkits and the Police Plan of Action on Inclusion and Race.
• West Mercia Police victim satisfaction and confidence survey outcomes.
• The Police and Crime Plan (The Safer West Mercia Plan) and its DEI related objectives.
• A range of staff surveys including an OPCC-led survey and those with external benchmarking benefits such as the Durham
University National Wellbeing and Inclusion Survey 2019 and the 'Speak up' (Right Conversation) survey.
• Workforce composition (equality) data over a 5 year period in relation to protected characteristics, by rank and grades.
• Feedback and insight from accountability and performance reviews with the Police and Crime Commissioner which have
helped identify workforce themes and patterns we need to address.
• Recommendations from Inspections, Legitimacy reviews (PEEL – Police effectiveness, efficiency and Legitimacy reviews).
• The priorities and work streams set out in our People Strategy and Delivery plans.
• Data on key policing activities such as Stop & Search, Use of Force.
• Ongoing consultation and engagement with our Independent Advisory Groups.

Engagement and feedback from community partnerships

(on issues such as hate crime).
• In future we will also be using established national Equality Standard tools (e.g. the Stonewall Index; National Equality Standard and others) to undertake gap-analyses to further inform strategic priorities and action plans.
• Our Equality Impact Assessments will allow us to identify issues for ongoing monitoring and change, to inform our strategic delivery plans.
• Our Gender Pay Gap Report findings.

- New ideas and good practice recommendations that will emerge from our Peer Review work on DEI (organised through the College of Policing, March – April 2021).

Applying learning from research.

There is ongoing work by the NPCC portfolio holders, the College of Policing and Durham University to identify interventions that would improve inclusivity in policing nationally and West Mercia police will be taking these
forward. In addition, it is vital that we take into account and learn from national public reviews of equality and inclusion topics – and particularly those which highlight ongoing race (minority ethnic) disproportionality within the Criminal Justice System.

These are issues upon which we must collaborate with criminal justice system and other partners. These include the findings and recommendations from the Lammy Review, the Home Affairs Select Committee and its recently published report (November 2020) Black People, Racism and Human Rights.

This strategy encompasses within its scope of the NPCC Plan of Action on Inclusion and Race.

My same observations apply here, as they did beneath the above 'Foreword'. The sad part about the whole of the document, not just the two introductory summaries above, is that they have nothing at all to do with the actual physical carrying out of practical policing, yet they are so overwhelmingly large. Surely all that was required in any annual report or objectives set is to acknowledge that: -

'Having signed up to the content of a 2018 National Police Chief Council document concerning the strategy on delivering Diversity, Equality an Inclusion, West Mercia Police has fully set in motion in every sense, the advice contained in that document so far as it concerns the employment and policing of its officers and support staff'.

That statement should, in my view, be sufficient and accepted by any reader and I cannot see, unless with any challenges, that evidence is required to prove that the statement is correct.

It is of course, the end product of the policing activity which should not suffer and be improved upon. It is this which I contend seriously requires improvement. My eyes therefore lit up when I saw mention of a 'Policing Charter' which also can be viewed under that 'key' quoted above. This was written by an Assistant Chief Constable Rachel Jones, and I was pleased to see a more refreshing and understandable style. However, what mystifies me is that having read it, I understand from what she says, that she is totally committed to Community Policing but we only have to look about us and be aware of that contained in the media or speak to friends, relations or neighbours, to realise that the quality of policing the community, especially the prevention and investigation of crime, has taken a huge nose-dive.

We have now appeared to have given up on the more purposeful policing of our communities, should this be aimed at the public, then they are not going to believe it unless some positive action is provided to corroborate what she promises. TV news now informs us that chief officers of police will direct that their police will attend every report of crime received from this time onwards. WOW! Gone are the days when if an officer did not attend a crime immediately, they would be liable to have been put on a disciplinary fizzer! It is these sorts of promises which must be seen to be honoured and might well start a resurgence that brings the community a little closer to the police.

It would not even be safe these days to park a marked police car on the 'not so law-abiding estates' to allow its occupants to patrol them. Should that even happen, the dialogue or relationships between those police and the community, would more than likely now be hostile as opposed to the friendly nature existing when community police were known by the inhabitants and when the regular officers patrolling, knew the members of the community. But that pain must be borne before anything positive can be expected. The previous confidence they might have had with the police which took many years to cultivate and develop, will now have been shattered and it is that which needs to be repaired. The very fact that no longer do uniform police want to join the ranks of the CID thus causing direct entry to the CID to be advertised, is surely an indication as to the situation now existing. More on that later but whatever Police Force inspections say about them, it is the categories relating to the 'Investigation of Crime', 'Responding to the public' and the 'Good use of resources' which will be viewed by the public to be the most important categories which now appear to be failing.

The members of our communities want to know about such matters and not about the contents of these 'gobbledegook' contracts written in 'Woke' language and topics which do far less to directly benefit the local police or the communities they are supposed to serve. I suggest that the repair of morale which I am told is very low and the competitive spirit among the 'troops', whether they be *sustainable, holistic, joined up, creative or whatever other gobbledegook adjective is applied to them,* is important and I do not see that producing such statements will affect those things at all.

6. Community Policing (Or The Lack Of It)

As suggested with the above title, I am of the view that we have lost our community policing initiatives and with it, the respect and confidence once held by those community members in our policing of them. We have given way to vile and generally, bad public behaviour and appear more interested in automatic speeding and parking fines than most forms of active policing.

I have seen two chief constables on TV recently promising that they would in effect, give 100% to getting back to policing with the community. They are naïve in my estimation because, apart from admitting that they were not policing the community in the first place, in any event, we have lost far too much ground in that respect to ever regain it. Sadly, I am of the strong opinion that we shall limp on using crutches, sticking plasters and the above type of objectives until someone radically grips the problem and gets us back to the pure and simple basics of coppering on the ground and not on paper or in cars.

It took the Covid 19 Pandemic to provide that flickering light with a little hope that our communities had not totally lost the spirit of togetherness. I was luckier than most because living in a rural village facilitated me walking out for probably more periods than most in urban areas. We formed little 'chat groups' who would stand in a circle on street corners making sure that the gaps between us were adhered to and that there was space on the other side of the road to allow passing pedestrians to pass by. I spoke to numerous people I had never spoken to before. It was not long before we had set up a volunteer scheme of those who were willing to shop for those who felt unsafe. There were so many volunteers that it became necessary to divide them up into sectors with a supervisor in each to administer and delegate the volunteers in each group. In addition, a weekly newsletter was produced which provided news about the latest situation as well as a few jokes and quizzes to boot. We called it the' Crowle Chat'.

So, this was community spirit raised from the dead in a matter of a couple of weeks. It came together because of harvesting volunteers, news, individual skills and the camaraderie of togetherness, so why could not that be applied to produce the emphasis required to increase confidence and contact between our police and the communities which they have appeared to have abandoned.

I have wondered since whether the game now is to produce these gobbledegook statements as just the words that are required to be said and then read by those in higher echelons who the police need to convince.

At my age, I often wonder if I have suddenly become a grumpy old man. My grandchildren think I have and one of them gave me the 'GRUMPY OLD GIT' socks for Christmas 2021 to prove it! So, they are probably correct! There are plenty who would subscribe to that notion and so I must admit to being pleased when I experience similar moans coming from other quarters. I draw some comfort in those few experiences – so perhaps I am not alone after all. One such person happens to be another retired chief superintendent colleague of mine, Philip Flower who I have never met or communicated with. He retired from the Metropolitan Force and the below is entirely his views which so closely, are in tune with my own. This is unusual as I have often blamed the Met. for most of our ills and would advocate it being split up. However, I have no compunction about repeating his views in total below. He was fortunate enough to have had his moans published in the Daily Mail newspaper (I know – so it must be correct!!) which is how I became acquainted with them. The first of such articles was published on 3rd February 2020 which was sparked by Mr Flower concerning two terrorist attacks in London, one being the attack on London Bridge. I include it below verbatim but without the images which accompanied the text.

Police will AGAIN feel utterly let down by the judiciary: PHILIP FLOWER says there is a wider problem of maintaining the morale of officers charged with keeping the public safe from these maniacs.

Boris Johnson has promised to put an end to soft sentencing and the early release of convicted terrorists – but I fear yesterday's bloody events on the streets of south London show the hollowness of politicians' words over the decades. At first glance, this looks alarmingly like a repeat of the London Bridge attack last year. Then, the perpetrator, Usman Khan, 28, had been released halfway through a 16-year sentence. Mr Johnson insisted lessons had been learned and would be acted upon. However, the record of recent years speaks differently. Politicians promise to take the fight to the judiciary, but they tend to retire hurt in the face of a confected clamour about human rights. As many as 40 of the 264 fanatics convicted of Islamist-inspired terrorism between 1998 and 2015 had their sentences reduced on appeal. At least seven have been jailed again since their release or had to return to prison for breaking licence conditions, including some caught spreading hate online or trying to travel to join Islamic State. After his release, Khan went on to kill two Cambridge graduates last year. Then, the perpetrator, Usman Khan, 28, had been released halfway through a 16-year sentence Yesterday's attacker seems also to have been a convicted terrorist who had been released, and was under close surveillance from the plain-clothes armed police who shot him when he launched his deranged assault.

As a retired senior police officer involved in containing terrorist and other threats during a 40-year career, I want to tell you of the intense frustrations that will be felt today across British policing. They will feel utterly let down by the judicial system. When I was a constable, I could arrest and process a suspect in an hour, maximum. Today, it takes a day or more. The police are mired in bureaucracy, while the judicial system has become an institutional cloud-cuckoo land.

As a society, we have to decide how to deal with terrorist suspects. It takes around 32 police officers to maintain around-the-clock surveillance of a single terror suspect. It is insane to attempt to maintain this level of supervision of the thousands of individuals known to be of interest to the security services and counter-terrorism police. It seems as though the Streatham perpetrator was being watched by armed police, yet still he managed to stab shoppers.

I am proud and relieved that we are not a totalitarian society, but at what cost do these liberties come? If we are to release convicted terrorists from jail early, then we would have to recruit thousands and thousands more police to oversee them, which of course will never happen because there is not enough money and we would find that level of intrusion unacceptable in a free society.

There is a wider problem of maintaining the morale of the officers charged with keeping the public safe from fanatics. Bluntly, how would you feel if you were told to keep track of known terrorists who have been released from prison to satisfy the politically correct assumptions of our justice system?

I remember a few years ago arriving at work when my junior officers seemed dispirited. I asked them what was wrong. They explained that the night before they had arrested a robbery suspect. He was 14, a refugee from Somalia, and entirely unconcerned by the consequences of his crime. He said he had grown up with an AK-47 in his hand and was not remotely scared of anything the Metropolitan Police could throw at him. I worry about this point more than any other. The police of course have to respect the law and the courts, and accommodate individuals from other countries and cultures. But the police and security services are fighting this domestic and global terrorism threat with one hand behind their backs. Or to put it another way, they are going on to the pitch in their cricket whites while the opposition is firing automatic rifles around their ears. There is another factor here. When I retired from the Metropolitan Police a few years ago, I told the Commissioner that what I feared most in my retirement was the prospect of murderous attacks from lone-wolf terrorists.

Yesterday's attack seems likely to have been at root what we in law enforcement tend to refer to as 'suicide by cop'. With their fake suicide vests, terrorists like the one yesterday in Streatham – and Usman Khan on London Bridge – seem to be asking to be shot dead. This is a relatively new and difficult policing challenge. In my day, counter-

terrorism tended to mean the threat from the IRA, plus some relatively minor aggravation from animal rights extremists. But those people wanted to fight for their causes, not necessarily die for them as a weird, self-sacrificial, futile gesture. The lone wolf is different. In counter-terrorism, intelligence is always the first line of defence. This could come from informants, colleagues, worried family members, and banks monitoring financial transactions. The lone wolf generally eschews any of these social interactions, so is much harder to track. Too often, he (and it is almost always a male) will be a low-achiever whose mental health has been compromised by drug use. He probably does not have a job, but is paid state benefits that enable him to sit alone at home, endlessly scouring poisonous material on the internet. He probably does not have a girlfriend and may well be estranged from his family. He is fundamentally disconnected from society and any social group.

When I talk to former colleagues still serving in the police, they say they worry more about the scores of home-grown would-be mass-murderers sitting in their bedsits scouring the internet than any direct threat from IS forces in Syria or Iraq. The challenge for us is how to engage with these people and take them out of the grip of their blind hatred. And to ensure that, if we have identified them and found them guilty, they are never released on the streets to maim and kill, as has tragically happened on too many occasions.

Funny, but unlike those 'woke' police publications I have dwelled on above, I can easily understand every sentence and paragraph of this above item. What Phil Flower describes in relation to the threat of terrorism was far from being on my agenda although as head of the Operations Department much of my time was taken up with arranging our defences against IRA attacks and as such, I became qualified as a hostage negotiator at the Metropolitan Police Training School, Hendon.

It was interesting to read that the defence against the IRA was at one time, most of what he was involved in but that the terrorism he recently fought, had spread to those other Syria, Iraq and 'loan wolf' threats. I wonder how long it will be for these types to spread to our counties where, due to the absence of community policing, they may now feel more under the radar? It is his reference to the mixed up and sad 'lone wolfs' of this world who, without social interactions of any kind, are difficult if not impossible to identify and track down. That situation will exist in our rural communities now unless we can reunite our police with those communities.

With the parole system and time off for good behaviour placed to one side, I often wonder what is it, or more importantly, who is it that can overturn a sentence handed out by judges? The 'lone wolves' he describes would probably always fall into the 'good behaviour' classification which might earn them remission. But anyway, these were always viewed as 'good behaviour' types and not gang members for it would be them who were sitting alone making their bombs or otherwise building up an armoury to perform vile acts of terrorism.

So, I would like to ride on the back of Mr. Flower's gripes. The way we policed prior to being mobilised in 1967 was very much different and I contend would vastly assist in the identification of those he calls 'Lone Wolves'. The local bobby would chat to the locals, and it would not be long before the 'odd ball' living at number 10 or wherever, would be the subject of their conversation. Where did he come from? Who is he? Etc. All that intelligence which would merely stem from having a chat, is now lost.

So let us fast forward and yet again, catch up with Mr Flower's more recent moans which again, accord so closely with my own. This was published again in The Daily Mail but on 25th August 2022, not so long ago.

"Why I despair for policing today: We need an urgent reset to restore order in the face of anarchy, writes former Chief Superintendent PHILIP FLOWER"

"Like everyone else in the country, I was shocked to hear about the appalling shooting of nine-year-old Olivia Pratt-Korbel in Liverpool on Monday night. For a child to be killed by a gun-wielding hitman chasing his prey into a

family home is a damning indictment of the state of society and modern policing.

Indeed, when I see the lawlessness rampant on Britain's streets, I fear we are descending into anarchy. Only 24 hours before Olivia's murder, council worker Ashley Dale, 28, was shot dead in the garden of her home less than two miles away. Meanwhile, we are in the grip of a nationwide knife-crime epidemic, and the Met is investigating 67 murders in London so far this year.

Across the country, senior officers appear to have completely lost sight of their basic role: to catch and deter criminals. Their junior colleagues, the products of a woke education system, often have totally unrealistic notions of what their job entails. They are deployed without appropriate training — and often behave in ways that shame the force. Increasingly, policing resembles a political activity. Some officers appear to regard painting their faces and dancing at Pride festivals, or taking the knee in solidarity with the hard-Left's Black Lives Matter movement, as their duty — instead of keeping the peace.

With the exception of murder investigations and pointless arrests over 'offensive' comments on social media, every aspect of policing has broken down. Drug-dealing, burglaries, car theft, dangerous driving, mass shoplifting raids and all kinds of other crime seems to go increasingly unchecked.

It isa shocking situation, and I am afraid it is getting worse. Videos posted online in recent days reveal that all kinds of crime are becoming ever more brazen. On Tuesday night, masked men fought each other with machetes in Leeds.

On Sunday, a screaming mob of about 50 young people stormed and looted a McDonald's restaurant in Nottingham, abusing and threatening staff, robbing the premises and filming themselves while they did so. An 'investigation' is supposedly under way, although no arrests have been reported.

Another film doing the rounds yesterday showed two muggers setting on a couple in broad daylight in London's Mayfair before leaping into a car and driving off. They did not care that neighbours were yelling at them, filming them and threatening to call 999.

The possibility that any police officers were within shouting distance, or would do anything about the crime if they could, was virtually zero — and the robbers knew it. Nearby at Hyde Park Corner on Sunday, two thieves on mopeds attempted to mug a man in a Bugatti supercar — and were again filmed while doing so. They were probably trying to snatch his wristwatch: 67 watch thefts were reported in the capital last month, more than two a day.

The litany continues. In Oxford Street, a gang of youths jumped and stomped over a Ferrari, simply because they could, while others rampaged into a sweets superstore and grabbed everything they wanted.

Gang attacks like these are now commonplace across the country, and videos uploaded to Twitter and YouTube show the teenage thieves rarely bother to cover their faces. Why would they? The chances of arrest and prosecution are vanishingly small. Crimes that would have ended with a spell in borstal 40 years ago are now routinely ignored.

Shamefully, recorded crime in England and Wales is now at a 20-year high, according to figures released last month by the Office for National Statistics. Some 6.3 million crimes were reported to police in the year to March 2022, with rape and other sexual offences, violence against the person and stalking and harassment all at record highs.

Amid this tsunami of human misery, just 5.6 per cent of offences reported to police led to a suspect being charged or summonsed — a new low.

As recently as 2014-2015, some 16 per cent of reported offences led to a suspect being charged. That figure has collapsed.

Without the police taking dangerous criminals off the streets, the fabric of society begins to fray. And that is what we are beginning to witness.

Like my former colleagues in the force, and like many serving officers today, I feel anger and despair at this terrible situation. And the increasingly woke mindset of some police is scarcely helping matters.

Which leads me to the farcical spectacle seen at Lincoln's annual Pride festival last Saturday. Four officers in shirtsleeves danced the Macarena, waving their arms and jumping on the spot in a synchronised display that had evidently taken some rehearsal.

'All fun down at Lincoln Pride,' crowed the force's Twitter account. Even when the video was denounced as embarrassing, Lincoln's Chief Constable Chris Haward could not see anything wrong with it.

'Pride is one of the many wonderful community events we are there to police,' he said, 'but also to allow people to look behind the uniform and see who we are.'

Toe-curling nonsense. The uniform is exactly what the public should see. It ought to inspire respect and represent probity. Yet, as I see it, growing numbers of police are disgracing their uniforms by behaving in utterly inappropriate ways while wearing them.

A number of forces have plastered their cars in the rainbow livery of the Pride movement, while at least one officer has been pictured with his policeman's helmet painted in rainbow hues. In a sense, this tiresome virtue-signalling would not matter if the police were doing their essential work keeping the streets safe for minorities. But they are failing to do so.

According to figures obtained by the Vice news website, in the past five years alone reports of homophobic hate crimes almost tripled from just over 10,000 in 2016-17 to almost 27,000 in 2021-22.

Several horrifying 'gay-bashings' have taken place, with innocent gay men hospitalised.

If the police truly wanted to 'reach out' to the gay community, that is what they would be tackling, instead of parading empty gestures with a rainbow flag. Britain's economy is in freefall. With fuel prices spiralling out of control and inflation predicted to soar above 18 per cent, protests this winter are a safe bet.

A few lawless, aggressive people could easily escalate these peaceful protests into looting and violence, just as they did in 2011, when thousands rioted across England and five people died.

When the police are no longer seen as a genuine deterrent, some people will feel emboldened to act beyond the law. And Britain's policing deterrent has worsened severely since those riots over a decade ago.

So, I fear for the safety of our streets this winter. Radical action is needed. My proposal is for a royal commission to examine every aspect of the police and redefine its purpose, with a shake-up at every level including how to keep politics out of policing.

Britain cannot continue to be a country where dealers are free to sell drugs in every park and street corner, where break-ins are routinely ignored, and where police officers disgrace their uniform by dancing at political marches.

I was deeply proud to be a copper. Now I am ashamed of what the police have become."

Why don't you say what you really think Phil? Oh, how sad it was whilst reading Mr Flower's description of the lawlessness involved in those incidents of moronic behaviour, all committed because they could be committed without detection. The only difference between retired Chief Superintendent Flower and myself is that he served in the Metropolitan Police where these things are more prevalent than in Herefordshire and Worcestershire but believe you me, where police failings are equally experienced and witnessed. This cancerous behaviour is bound to spread.

As a footnote to his scribblings, he describes the 'Just Stop Oil' brigade on the M25 as a small group of self-indulgent environmental protesters. He said,

> **"Put simply, the continuing scenes of motorway mayhem was an embarrassment to British policing".**

With both Phil and I being retired and of the same rank, we have no compunction in 'shouting our mouths off' at the injustices we see and perceive today. But where are the voices of the chief constables on the top landings of police headquarters? Why do they remain silent and play along with this Wokism we now suffer?

In addition to the fear of falling out with their Police and Crime Commissioners, not to speak of the inspectorate and the Home Office which so easily could result in them to lose their jobs, I have come to realise that they are all of a generation and a half younger than us and will have never witnessed the community policing initiatives of our days. So, for that reason and having hopefully set the policing scene where we are today in comparison, I would now like to flash back to the period in my policing life when I contend that things were not so bad as they are today. It all seemed a struggle even then, but goodness gracious me, I never ever believed that our lawlessness would ever drop to such low levels as Mr Flower describes.

This may take some time, but I implore readers to bear with me whilst I now go back to describe in plain English and without any gobbledegook language, what life was like by the public and their police before such mayhem was so commonplace. Having looked at the past will be of help when bringing us up to date with a comparison. I will not shirk with dealing with the wrongdoings of the past in future chapters. However, I would advocate that the straightforward compliance with the oaths we took when joining the police, is sufficient to ensure that we could get on with the job of protecting the peace and the prevention and detection of crimes committed. It is important therefore to look to the future, we flash back to examine how we evolved, a period from which will not have been experienced by members of the force today.

7. Flashback to Early Experiences

My acceptance into the police force in 1960 were the days when not so much emphasis was placed on the education of those being recruited. Failing the eleven plus examination and later, in senior school, failing English Grammar examination bears testament to that, the latter is no doubt the reason why I struggle over writing books! Fine! I was without a GCE but was told that all this was not so important because employment of some description or other, would always be available. But how things have changed! Whilst university was never on the menu of any student at my senior school, their doors appear now, to have been considerably widened. That is a good thing!

I had no idea what I wanted to do but Dad told me that as I was tall and liked sports, the police would be a place where I could continue my sporting pursuits. There was none of the "I want to repay society" or "I want to help the community" etc. I just needed a job and here I am, as they say, the rest is history.

I was an only child but had a bunch of very good mates living nearby. We played football in the World Cup almost every day, but it was our coats that were the goal posts. We were without the Internet, computers, mobile phones, tablets (those you didn't swallow), gaming machines and most homes including my own, were, for a very long time, without a telephone, television and central heating. Letters were frequently written and exchanged by my family members who, because of my father's posting to a munitions factory in Hereford just prior to the war, were all living in other parts of England and Wales.

We had a full set of encyclopaedias but the only other connections we had with the outside world were newspapers and the wireless. Our wireless had wires, so I guess it was a radio and therefore not a wireless. The newspapers were of the cheap tabloid type, and I recall the first ones we took were the Daily Sketch.

Sport was my life and I remember my dad waking me up in the middle of the night to listen to some heavyweight boxing championship of the world usually taking place in the USA. The radio crackled and the transmissions were often lost at critical stages. He would constantly curse at the radio about this situation.

He was a poorly paid electrical engineer and was frequently on the sick list with emphysema. So, my mum had the need to work to help pay the mortgage for the house where I was raised in Hereford and in which they had first rented for many years and from which, by the way, I walked to my wedding with my best man, Barry Hayden.

On arriving home from school, I was able to play in the street with my mates whilst leaving the house unlocked. I could put my dinner on a saucepan and put it on the gas stove to heat up. I had watched my mother do this frequently, she put an upturned plate on top of the meal before lighting the gas stove. It was easy, so what could possibly go wrong? It was at my first attempt that when I returned a little later to consume it, the house was full of black smoke and the bottom of the saucepan had burned through. What a stink! It was of course, mum's fault for not telling me to put water in the saucepan!!! Duhhh; no wonder I didn't pass that eleven plus examination!

Even though crimes were committed, I rarely heard about instances of them as there was no fear of us being burgled. (Nothing much there anyway) Our parents did not appear to be worried about us being abducted or kidnapped when out of their sight and we were allowed to ride our bikes as far as we wished to nearby woods or even to the next town at Ross on Wye. This was fourteen miles away and along the very busy A49 trunk road.

We also often played by the river Wye at St Martins, only about a mile from home and some of us frequently returned home wet through or covered in mud from its banks after taking an unexpected slither down the bank. It could not have been because our parents did not care about us because I know they did, and all children of our age were 'let loose' in similar fashion. There was no fear.

The police in those days were just there. I suppose like everyone else; they generated a slight fear when in their presence, but I placed no other significance with anything to do with them. They were visible and I just did not want to cross their paths and in so far as I was concerned, they were employed to catch baddies and uphold the laws. I never took much notice of the police. They were burley men who would not take lip from anyone for fear of being clipped around the ear and or marched to your parents. The constables were very likely to know where you lived and who your parents were and what they did. And so, the unofficial contract between the community and police naturally evolved through a built-in fear of being caught and what might ensue if you were.

Little did I know that in years to come, the local copper, Bert Harding (we called him Uncle Bert) would get me into trouble with the chief constable of the day, Robert McCartney. Our little avenue, Dinedor Avenue was located

very near to the boundary fence of the military establishment, Bradbury Lines. This was occupied by a Boys Regiment then, but it became the first home of the 22nd Special Air Service Regiment (SAS) and it was later re-named Stirling Lines after the regiment's founder, Colonel David Stirling. The regiment has since moved to an ex-RAF station at Credenhill on the outskirts of Hereford, but its name, 'Stirling Lines' was transferred to it with the regiment.

Author circa 1954 aged 10 yrs.

Quite near to the edge of the barrack's boundary was a piece of land containing an empty, very large abandoned single story wooden hut which had been used as a NAFI for the occupants of the barracks during the war. It was surrounded by overgrown weeds, but our gang had forged a path around its circumference, and we used it as a race track. That is where we held the Olympics when we were not playing in the world cup.

The centre of the apex of the roof was what I can only describe as a metal chimney though it was not a chimney at all. It was like a box and would have been some sort of vent. I had climbed onto the roof and sitting astride the apex, I rhythmically banged on this box with both hands whilst imagining that this was my 'Tom- Tom' drum. It made a hell of a din!

I had the fright of my life when my mates shouted up to me that 'Uncle Bert' was heading for us. I slid down the roof very close to a corner of the building and jumped just as Bert rounded the corner. We collided and both fell to the ground. This obviously made him even angrier, and he marched me off to our house just about 100 yards away. My mates had scarpered leaving me to my destiny. I hasten to add that he did not give me a clout but when my dad arrived home from work, he went berserk, and I had a roasting as well as a 'clip'.

Uncle Bert was never promoted beyond sergeant, but it would have been about ten years later that he was employed in the force's Information Room where the whole shift comprised just one sergeant, one constable and a cadet. He was the sergeant, and you might have guessed that I had been thrown into working alongside him.

The three cadets employed in the building took it in turns to make the tea twice a day for all those employed at headquarters. This involved the brewing of two large brown tea pots, so I am guessing from memory that we were catering for around twenty people in all. What a difference that is compared with the hundreds now employed in the current West Mercia headquarters at Hindlip Hall. Having made the tea, it was necessary to enter the information room located opposite to the small kitchen and rest room where all gathered to drink it. All offices were informed that it was ready by using the intercom in the information room by repeatedly buzzing them in turn. This was the signal which signified, 'Tea Up'.

The intercom was in a corner of the Information room right next to the main switchboard. With reference to the photograph below, (circa 1962) the door leading into the room from across the kitchen was just to the left of the filing cabinets which I am working on. The switchboard and intercom were immediately opposite to that door and would have been near to the bottom right-hand corner of the photograph. It was one of those contraptions now seen in museums and included many torpedo type plugs on the end of cables which when lifted, came out of their individual holes to be placed in the allocated extension number to make a connection.

This was Herefordshire Constabulary's Force Operations Room, then called the Information Room. It shows Sergeant 116 Roberts (Tubby) and PC 32 Ernie Clinton, the only two members of staff employed in it apart from myself updating the nominal index of wanted or suspected criminals.

On entering the room, Bert was on the telephone, but I could see that flap number twelve was popping up and down.

I did not know how to operate the switchboard, but I knew that number twelve was the chief constable's extension so, with much trepidation, I answered it, and the chief gave me a telephone number which he wanted to be connected. I waited for Bert to come off his extension and then I gave him the number the chief had asked for which I had written on a piece of paper.

It was not long after, that all three of us cadets were summoned together to see the chief. His office was right next door to our 'General Office', but I had never seen inside it before other than what was on view from the open door. I can only speak for myself, but I was shaking in my boots. To my surprise, he never referred to me as the culprit but exclaimed that to forget about a call he had asked to be made, was simply not on and that from now on, until told otherwise, cadets would make the tea and not drink it!!

Bert Harding had obviously forgotten about his call, but I was too afraid to remonstrate with the chief and tell him. In any event, how we could make the tea and not drink some was beyond us and so the situation was soon back to normal. At that time, I had been winning many trophies with Hereford Rowing Club and so had become a blue-eyed boy with the chief who, when the HMI called, often used to parade me on the inspection to gloat in my successes on the river. I was back to being his 'blue eyed boy'!

So, that was our little county force of Herefordshire comprising three divisional headquarters at Hereford, Leominster, and Ross on Wye. There were other small towns included in these divisions and many village police stations. We were such a small force, that when we merged to form the West Mercia Constabulary, we consisted of 209 constables and sergeants, 10 policewomen and 2 war reservists. There were only 9 inspectors and 4 chief inspectors. With only four superintendents, one of those doubled as 'The Deputy Chief Constable'. The Chief Constable, Robert McCartney lost his job and became the Deputy Governor of the Tower of London. He was quite strict, and many said that it was a pity that he did not lose his head there! In addition, 23 civilian staff and 14 police cadets were also transferred. So, when a sergeant or above died, bereavement was often accompanied by joy in respect of the ensuing promotions that those deaths brought.

Recruitment has changed beyond recognition since I joined. It would be very doubtful indeed that I would have progressed as I did or even would have been recruited into the job today. We police with the consent of the community and it is only right and proper that we utilise the broadest spectrum of society possible, to police it. We need that microcosm of society but from what I now earn, that philosophy is very much in danger.

Policemen were invariably cartooned as overweight rotund, often red nosed characters possessing quite a capacity for many pints of ale. They were required to reach certain measurements in height and expanded chest dimensions. They would also almost always be wearing their helmet which added to them being regarded with respect, even though that may not have been earned.

In those early 1960s, one hardly ever seemed to hear of a promotion taking place but when they did, details rapidly circulated the force by word of mouth. Promotion was very much like waiting for dead men's shoes so being ambitious was hardly worthwhile. The likelihood of promotions coming your way, was very remote and if it did, you would have possessed exceptional qualities and even then, only when those dead men's shoes were made available.

Little did I realise that things were to change quickly in 1967 when the West Mercia Constabulary was formed, and many other constabularies were similarly amalgamated. There were more opportunities, but they were furthest from my mind.

8. Restrictions on Private Lives

'Police Accommodation'

When considering how I was going to construct this chapter, I wondered whether those intending to be recruited today, would have put up with what was suffered in the job at the time of and before my policing era.

Even in Victorian times, cottages in villages were supplied to police officers who were required to pay a rent. However, I am indebted to police historian Robert Bartlett who provided me with an excellent clip from an article headed 'Lord Normanby's Rules taken from *A History of Police in England and Wales" Critchley page 150* believed to have been written c1840, as follows: -

> *.......you were not in the police to earn good money. You were there because the pay was regular and consistent with in the long term a pension. Accommodation was provided though rent was to be paid; the married man had his vegetable garden. Rural police officers were often helped with the gift of eggs, vegetables, pheasants and rabbits the acceptance of which was likely to attract the disapprobation of senior officers but for many it helped feed the family.*

Nothing much changes then? Well, perhaps a little.

There are numerous articles to be found in local newspapers published in the 1930s which refer to the construction of village police stations as we knew them in the 1960s, which were built 30 years previously. However, in the context of this book, it is the more modern era that I am interested in which concerns the eventual selling of those police houses built immediately following the end of the last war.

In that context, I am indebted to another two members of the Police History Society, Pam Mills and Terence Gardner who, following my appeal, both provided me with copies of Home Office Circular 300/1944 dated 29th November 1944 headed 'Houses for Police in the Immediate Post War period'. This was sent to every Home Office chief constable and their chairmen of police authorities whose responsibility it was to find suitable land and issue tenders for such huge building operations.

I think it worthwhile for historical purposes that I include the full copy circular of it here but in an attempt to make it more readable, I have sliced it up to fit more comfortably into these pages: -

HOME OFFICE,
WHITEHALL,
S.W.1.
29th November, 1944

Sir,

HOME OFFICE CIRCULAR NO. 300/1944
Houses for police in the immediate post-war period

1. The Secretary of State has had under consideration the question of housing the members of the police forces in the immediate post-war period. As police authorities will appreciate, this will present some very difficult problems; the police, like the rest of the population, will suffer from the effects of the general housing shortage, and, particularly in the County forces, the problem may be made even more difficult by the need to station a constable in a particular locality in which adequate housing accommodation may not be available for him and his family. Another factor to be borne in mind is that when recruitment for the regular police is resumed it is likely that a high proportion of the recruits will be married men. The provision of adequate housing accommodation by the police authority will obviously make a significant contribution to the contentment, and therefore to the efficiency, of the police force and would be likely to affect materially the standard of recruit in the post-war period.

2. The Secretary of State would accordingly urge police authorities to take such steps as are possible, in consultation as necessary with the appropriate housing authorities, to ensure that members of the police force are adequately housed. This will not necessitate the provision of police houses as such for all members of the force, particularly in City and Borough forces.

3. The Secretary of State is not yet in a position to approve any proposals for the use of building labour or materials on permanent police housing schemes. Apart, therefore, from the measures referred to in paragraphs 5 and 7 below, all that can be done now is for police authorities to review requirements, in order to ensure that all necessary information may be available as soon as it is needed and that there is no avoidable delay in proceeding with building work when this is authorised.

4.   The Secretary of State fully appreciates the difficulty police authorities will find in attempting to make any detailed review of the post-war situation, having regard to the uncertainty there must be as to the probable post-war establishment of the police force, its geographical distribution over the police district and, in particular, the percentage of new recruits likely to be married. These are all points which provide a wide field for conjecture; the question of the probable strength and distribution of the forces can best be determined in consultation with the Chief Constable in the light of local circumstances and on the provisional basis of a strength roughly equivalent to the pre-war strength, and, as regards the last point, the Secretary of State would suggest that it would be unwise to assume that less than 50% of the new recruits will be married.

5.   Apart from the general review suggested in the previous paragraph there is one practical step which police authorities can take at this stage, namely the acquisition of sites at places where there is a clear indication that police houses will required in the immediate post-war period. In accordance with the Government's general policy, the Secretary of State will be prepared to approve the acquisition of sites at a value which is not in excess of that which would be payable in accordance with Part II of the Town and Country Planning Act 1944. Subject to this limitation, the Secretary of State would urge police authorities to acquire sites now in cases where it is clear that police houses will be needed in the post-war period. The police authority should, in future consult the Regional Planning Officer of the Ministry of Town and Country Planning and also the local planning authority as regards the general suitability of the site; and it will normally be convenient if the Secretary of State's approval of the purchase of sites is sought after the police authority have consulted the Regional Planning Officer and the local planning authority and have obtained the District Valuer's advice on the value of the site. Negotiations for the acquisition of sites should then as a rule be conducted by the District Valuer; if they are not, police authorities should not, without previous reference to the Secretary of State, enter into any agreement which would bind them to pay a price exceeding the District Valuer's recommendation or would impose upon them onerous conditions which have not been taken into account be him. Where it is desired that the purchase of sites should be financed by way of loan, the Secretary of State will offer no objection in appropriate cases, subject to the consent of the Minister of Health being obtained.

6.   The Secretary of State will keep police authorities informed of any material developments in the general housing plans of the Government which affect the particular problems of the police service, but in the meantime he would be glad if they would furnish him as soon as possible with an estimate (a) of the number of sites they propose to acquire and (b) of the number of new houses required under the following headings:-

(i)   the number of houses which will be required to replace houses at present rented but which are likely to be given up at the end of the war;

(ii)   the number required to replace existing houses which are definitely inadequate or unsatisfactory; and

(iii)   the number of houses which will be required in addition to those under (i) and (ii).

The figures under (b) (i) (ii) and (iii) should be only of houses which will have to be built. They should not include any suitable existing existing houses which the police authority propose to rent or purchase, but particulars of the latter should be given separately under the above headings.

7.   As regards the immediate future, there may be some emergency measures which police authorities can take which will be of value during the critical period with which police authorities will be faced until progress has been made with the general rehousing programme. Such measures would include the renting of houses for immediate occupation; or the acquisition of premises which can be adapted for occupation, e.g. by conversion into flats. Where the police authority desire to purchase such accommodation, the purchase price which the Secretary of State will be prepared to approved will be such as may be agreed by the District Valuer, who as a general rule should be asked to undertake the negotiations for purchase.

It may also be possible to arrange with the appropriate housing authority for a certain number of police officers to be accommodated in temporary factory-built houses, as and when these become available.

8.   Police Authorities will, in may cases, have to consider schemes for the provision or improvement of police station and administrative buildings, many of which have been postponed as a result of the war. Where such schemes involve the acquisition of sites the principles set out in this circular apply; as regards the prospect of there being building labour and materials available for these schemes, the Secretary of State appreciates that in many cases improvements in administrative buildings are urgently necessary in the interests of efficiency, but he feels sure that police authorities will agree that, in the absence of quite exceptional circumstances, the needs of the men must come first and that the provision of police houses must for the time being take precedence over administrative building schemes.

                I am, Sir,
                Your obedient Servant,

                          S.H. Baker.

The Clerk to the Police Authority,
The Chief Constable.

Further copies of the minutes of the Kent Standing Joint Committees concerning the whole planning and building processes were also included in Pam's research.

P.C. moves into 100th Kent police house

ALL MOD. CON., PLUS AN OFFICE AND A GARAGE

WHEN P.C. Richard Sugden and his family move into their new house, complete with office and garage, at St. Edith's Road, Kemsing, near Sevenoaks, today, the Kent County Police achieve something that gives much cause for satisfaction, shared by officials of several County Council Departments.

It marks the end of the untiring effort which has gone into the planning and construction of 100 new dwellings for police officers of Kent.

This important stage is, however, only the beginning of an ambitious programme approved by the Kent Police Authority and the Home Office, which aims at providing good, modern, attractive accommodation for almost 900 members of the County Force.

A further 100 houses are in the course of erection, many nearing completion.

" MINIATURE STATION "

The premises at Kemsing might aptly be described as a miniature police station, for the resident officer, P.C. Sugden, is equipped to deal promptly with anything which might crop up during his daily duty.

The size of the houses is limited by present building regulations to 1,000 square feet—about the size of a modern council house. They contain six rooms and are built to a standard design which incorporates a small heated cubicle for drying uniform.

The object of standardising is, of course, to minimise the domestic upset when officers are transferred from one station to another.

It is expected that the small office will prove a boon to the local constable and his "customers." Formerly, of course, he was obliged to receive all callers in his own home, but the new office will give him a measure of privacy and enable duty matters to be kept apart from home life.

In addition to the 100 standard houses already completed, the Kent Police Authority have purchased 18 new ordinary type dwellings since 1948 for housing police officers.

Clip dated 25 August 1950 –

The Kent Messenger & Gravesend Telegraph -

Pam had also sent me a clipping from the East Kent Times and Mail dated 6th September 1950 which confirmed that urban 'estate' houses were being built in the 1950s indeed her clip indicated that the 100th police house had just been constructed in Kent. It was this same house which also featured in the above clip from the Kent Messenger & Gravesend Telegraph of 25th August ,1950 which, as can be seen, had now been occupied by a PC Richard Sugden.

To bring us up to date, the below photograph is of a pair of semi-detached police houses in Newtown Road, Worcester. They were not in the best of condition, and we had moved there in April 1969 resulting from my promotion to sergeant. I guess I was so pleased about being promoted that I wasn't so concerned as my wife Jo. We had been moved from a smart police house in Hereford where we were only the second occupiers, yet here we were in this much older house, the one on the left, number 90. A detective constable and his wife occupied the right hand one and it was he who might have been deputed as the detective constable onto which each 'Panda Car Area' was supplied. (Not in Herefordshire as they were a near extinct breed or we did not have enough to share) It can be seen by the location of the windows that the houses mirrored each other.

Police Office Door

What is not so clear is that at ground level only, there is a flat roofed structure extending outward from the centre. This was designed and had been used as a police office by the Resident Beat Officer/s. It had not been occupied for over a year which indicated that it would indeed, have been in the 1967/68 era when Unit Beat Policing had been introduced. This is a more recent photograph which I took in 2016. What had been the heavy blue door into the office, was now brown. There had been two paths leading to the front doors, but the current owner has now reconfigured the front so as to provide car parking space which was not there when we were.

The house not having been occupied for well over a year, my tearful wife with our six-month-old baby daughter, went down to the telephone kiosk and summoned the assistance of her mother from Hereford. (Oh God!) This was in one of those 'not so salubrious estates' and still in tears, she came back to tell me that some women were in the shop in their slippers and with curlers in their hair! Oh dear, what grace had we fallen from!

Mother-in-law had arrived and we were throwing buckets of water over the glossy painted walls just to get the dust off them before giving it a good clean. The internal doors had been trimmed off at the bottom for God knows how many carpets to be fitted, that the water was flowing freely from one room to another. The garden too was in such an overgrown state.

It was not long after we had settled, that I received permission to move to another similar, but far more comfortable police house in a better area. It must be remembered that apart from natural changes occurring in society, in those years gone by, certainly in the early 1960s, police recruits were very hard to attract in county forces. I now wonder if that had anything to do with the conditions imposed which hopefully had improved a great deal since Lord Mornanby's days.

For the information of those reading this who were not 'police family', forces were continually advertising for recruits, but it was not a job that attracted sufficient applicants. The job did not pay very well and there were height restrictions which automatically negated quite a percentage of people who would have otherwise joined. I had heard of potential recruits wearing three pairs of socks just to ensure that they reached the magic height of 5'10".

One of the few attractions to the job was that this type of accommodation would be provided to recruits and if there were not sufficient police owned houses available, then a rent allowance based on the rateable value of a 'moderate' police house would be paid to assist the payment for rented accommodation. This was called 'Rent Allowance'.

Many recruits had either served in the military through the mandatory 'National Service' scheme or who had been signed on for years before and / or after national service ended in 1960. As we discovered, the houses provided were not always the best. Some were without bathrooms and even in my day, two rows of dwellings in what was DeLacey Street (Now demolished to make way for new police station) which adjoined the old police station in Hereford comprised completely of old terraced police houses, about seven or eight on each side. Many of my friends living today recount how they were forced to bathe in tin baths in front of open fires. When not in use, the baths were hung on the walls of the small yards at the rear of them where the outside toilets were also located. Some were overlooked by neighbours, and this was why DeLacey Street was nick-named, 'Urinal View.'

The main point of raising this here was that police regulations then stipulated that you were to live wherever the chief constable said you were to live. You were not given any options. Police houses were scattered all over these cities, towns, and villages and although there were some positioned in better areas than others, it was those built in what later became ghettoes or run-down crime infested estates, that were very handily positioned to being occupied by the same officers who were employed as community constables on them. It goes to prove how far sighted they were in the 1950s to build police accommodation on those estates. That Home Office Circular 300/1944 says it all.

This situation was quite acceptable to those officers working and living on their estates. They were only too pleased to have been given a free house and it is the selling of them which represents my major criticism of the policing strategies of today. At a stroke, we lost the policing initiative and handed over the estates to the 'baddies' living on them.

One might have questioned, "How dare a chief constable stipulate where his officers must live"? However, all were quite pleased that they were given such accommodation and, in any event, those coming from a military background were used to living in similar military accommodation and as a bonus, could accept discipline more easily to those being recruited from life elsewhere.

Initial police training was conducted over a thirteen-week course at a 'Regional Police Training Centre' where drill and saluting 'officer ranks' would be very much accustomed by those ex-servicemen and ex-police cadets who were also 'drilled' during their cadet training.

The training centres contained ex-guardsmen now in the police sergeant rank who were acting as 'Sergeant Majors' conducting compulsory drill sessions. How often have you seen such a salute these days? Indeed, one might ask, how often do you even see a police officer on foot these days?

However, the question posed about how chief constables could dictate where their officers must live, is so easily answered. This was simply the 'payback' for being provided with police accommodation, or the payment of a rent allowance. Provision was contained in legislation and the Statutory Instruments called 'Police Regulations' empowering chief constables to direct their officers to live wherever they wanted them to live. That was it!

Of course, for that reason, police officers were not allowed to purchase their own houses in which to reside without their chief constable's consent, even in the unlikely event that they could afford such a purchase. I want to make it clear that this power was not questioned by the officers who were often posted from pillar to post around the various counties. They joined knowing these requirements but the attraction of being provided with accommodation or a rent allowance was so great that, coupled with a good pension to be paid on retirement, this restriction on our private lives could be tolerated without complaint.

The disadvantages of this situation were only relaxed towards the end of an officer's service and many officers were forced to include their names on the council house waiting list so that they had somewhere to live when their retirement day arrived. But the restrictions on our private lives did not end there. The power of chief constables ruling over our domestic lives was huge and being able to stipulate where we lived did not just mean from within the town or village we were from or where we were first posted to. We could be directed to live in any of the locations within the county being policed. In addition, posting officers to far flung places without any operational requirement, was often used as a punishment.

It was towards the end of this era prior to the selling of these police houses that a few of them were used to house many single officers of the same sex. My own son-in-law recounts that he was among some who lived in police houses at Spetchley Road, Worcester.

Chief officers were not only able to stipulate where we lived but for those single men who were thinking of marrying, police regulations of the day provided for them to have our prospective wives vetted. They needed to be satisfied that they carried no criminal or moral 'baggage' in that they or their families were not of ill repute.

There were other impositions which were linked into the above powers and one of them stipulated that you or your close family could not be engaged in any business enterprise. As a single man though courting my future wife at Hereford, I had been posted to the market town of Ledbury where I had been found suitable lodgings in which to live. With not much ever happening at Ledbury, my first objective was to get a posting back to Hereford but that didn't happen for a while and then it was only because my father became very ill, and my mother required supporting both financially and physically.

In addition, it was not uncommon for single male police officers to marry female police officers. It was an unbelievable instruction that these couples were not permitted to work on the same shifts as each other. This was felt so unreasonable that eventually, many cases were reconsidered but of course, that power remained within the reach of the Chief Officers of those days.

Like many other counties, Herefordshire was largely rural and so many, if not most villages, were equipped with their own police station which doubled as a residence, or rather it was a residence which doubled as a police station as described above among those built in the 1930s and later. I recall that every village police station's notice board had a coloured picture of a Colorado Beetle on it. This was an insect which had been responsible for ruining certain crops but it became a humorous topic to recount that it was often the only photograph depicting a creature that was 'WANTED' on these notice boards, yet no one had actually seen one for years! Heaven helps you though, if the inspector called and there was not a Colorado beetle displayed on your notice board.

And so, this policy of providing police accommodation in our villages and on more urban estates, ensured that we had a police presence in all urban and rural communities. Again, both the chief officer and all (or most) of his officers were content with where they lived and worked. Above all, the communities being policed were content. In the rural areas, they had been given a sheriff of their village and he, (and later, she) became important fulcrums of society resident in them.

On 7th December 1970, we moved from that 2nd police house in Worcester, to 'The Sergeants House' in the village of Alfrick some miles into the deep rural area of Worcestershire where I was charged with supervising not only the constable living next door to us in that village but other rural village police stations which in effect, circled just outside the outer perimeter of the estates on the outskirts of Worcester. So having cut down my experiences in the rural section station, that nicely covers my 'beat house' experiences.

Except that in our rural beat house, there were cattle in the field at the foot of our garden and one day, we became concerned at them walking around in what appeared to be a swamp. The smell was not pleasant either! Being almost 'city slickers' we had not realised that our sewage was being disposed of into a septic tank and it obviously wanted emptying. This was duly reported and a company from Evesham arrived with a tanker to empty it. It was a very hot day and they had spent hours locating the manhole cover and emptying the tank.

These were the days when I brewed my own beer, and in sympathy for them due to the dirty nature of the work on this very hot day, I offered the pair of them a drink of my beer. It went down without touching the sides and so they had another. Yes, those were the days when you could drink alcohol and drive, so long as you were not obviously drunk. I was not present when they finally left but later, on my return to the station, I found one of our brand-new double wrought iron gates lying on the ground. The tanker could only have left through that 'exit' gate, and I guessed that it had brushed against it on leaving. I duly reported that some vehicle must have knocked it off.

The restrictions on our private lives could never linger on in a more modern society which was becoming increasingly mindful of human rights. Police pay received a boost through a Royal Commission conducted by Sir Henry Willink QC in 1960 and then in 1977, a further salary injection was provided in a review conducted by Lord Edmund Davies. Although no police officer was going to be rich just on their pay, they were then more likely to afford to purchase their own property if they were allowed to. However, a decade earlier, the structure and organisation of police forces had already made huge changes.

Our West Mercia Constabulary was formed from the amalgamation of four police forces, Herefordshire, Worcestershire, Shropshire, and the Worcester

City force. From the 'Local Authority' perspective of funding the police, Herefordshire and Worcestershire had already combined to form a unitary authority. However later in 1994, a new Police Act established the power of Police Authorities to own its own property and to levy a police rate onto local citizens.

The accommodation arrangements as described above had not been the same for recruits joining the small 'City' or 'Borough' forces. Their boundaries were so small that they were not in fear of being posted from one end of a county to another. They were therefore permitted to buy their own houses and so, this attracted more recruits resulting in their establishment always being full. Police accommodation was however, also provided in these smaller forces, because they were required to be filled by officers working in the locations where they lived. (Resident Beat Officers) They were also occupied by other officers who weren't able to afford to purchase their own. But it was because they were allowed to purchase their own, that these houses were only occupied on a short-term basis, until their occupants could manage to move to their own. The rapid turnover of their occupants meant that their condition was not of a very high standard as we had discovered.

It was at about this time when many of the older long serving patrol sergeants on the shifts were retiring and experience became diluted when youngsters (including myself) began to take their places. On reflection, I believe that this was the era when policing and its leadership and supervision began to slacken. Many of these men had left the military after the war and had now retired from their police service by taking their 25- and 30-years pensions.

This was also not too long after our policing strategy had changed from 'foot patrol' to riding around in Panda cars equipped with mobile radios. That was when we thought that all our Christmases had arrived at once, but more on that later at the appropriate time.

9. Organisation and Structure

'The Basics'

The changes made did not upset the status quo immediately in that we were to maintain the policing of every inch of land in our villages, on our estates and in the countryside, but it changed the way we did it. But little did we know that this was to be the thin edge of the wedge that saw the last of our real community policing.

Three separate strati were used. These involved the central urban town or city areas, then on their outskirts, there would be the large housing estates or industrial areas patrolled by 'Resident Beat Officers' (RBOs) who worked on the beats in which they lived. Depending on the location, these RBOs in other areas were referred to as Local Beat Officers (LBOs) but they did the same job.

Finally, as I have described at Alfrick above, where these estates met the rural areas, each part would be covered by a village police officer who again, would be resident at his village police station. In a few cases. villages small enough might have needed to share one constable. They worked in conjunction with neighbouring village bobbies to cover for days off but when on duty, due to there being a pro-rata less density of calls to attend, they were given a 24-hour responsibility.

What better method of policing could be adopted? Yet we freely gave it all away to succumb to what became known as 'fire brigade policing' which by its very nature, was completely reactive and completely unresponsive to relationships which would have been hitherto constructed through years and years of community policing. I live in a village now which thirty odd years ago was policed by a constable residing in such a police house. I knew him well and even today; I meet older residents who were living here then and they can all remember PC Bob Mason and tell me of stories about him. That says it all. This simple structure of policing our communities prior to the death of community policing, is perhaps easier explained by using my basic ring doughnut diagram below. I realise that it does not look much like a ring doughnut but imagine that the central blank area is the hole in the centre of it. This represents the larger urban areas, the towns and cities patrolled around the clock by three shifts of police officers delegated to work individual beats commencing at 6am, 2pm and 10pm. (There were also variations)

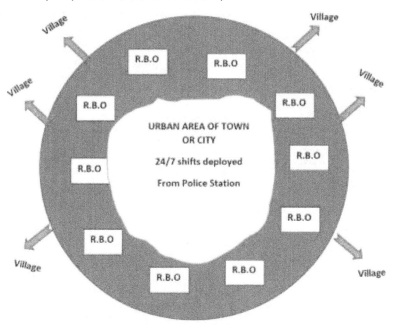

The eating part of the doughnut (shaded) circling the urban town and city centres will be totally covered by Resident Beat Officers (RBOs). These officers will be housed in police authority owned houses on estates mostly built post war as per the 1944 Home Office Circular. They together, ensured that the doughnut ring was covered by their combined patrols. Naturally, they were most useful when housed in those problem areas often requiring police attention. Finally, as denoted by the word 'Village', the total area would be covered by village bobbies working from their own village stations who patrolled on cycles or later, on low powered motorcycles.

This 'doughnut' strategy would be duplicated throughout every Division thus ensuring that every inch of them would be covered by a police patrol who would be responsible for whatever happened on their beat. They 'owned' it and I contend that it was this 'ownership' which created a fine method of policing and an excellent relationship with those who resided and worked on those beats.

We must now realise how important this new 'Panda Car' policing strategy called 'Unit Beat Policing' would be, when viewing the changes made to the service provided to our communities. Whilst the Resident Beat Officers (RBOs) were occupying police authority owned houses located on their beats, those working the inner city / town urban areas would normally comprise a mix of the younger recruit with more senior officers.

Many if not most, would also occupy police accommodation in those places but some would be renting their accommodation and being compensated through the payment of a rent allowance. These urban areas were also used to introduce new recruits from the training establishments who would first be accompanied by 'Parent Constables' showing them the ropes for, in my case anyway, six weeks.

The important point here is that this doughnut description meant that 100% of towns and cities were being policed by foot / cycle patrols with officers assigned to specific beats. In the urban areas, on night duty, apart from their general street patrol, officers were expected to check the doors of every shop and business on their beats. This was a twice nightly duty if they were lucky and not overloaded with the administration required following the arrest of those taken into police custody.

A full register of the contact details of every premises was maintained at police stations and when a business premises was discovered to be 'insecure, the 'key holder' would be contacted to attend the premises and an appropriate entry would be made in the 'Insecure Premises' register. It would be unusual not to discover one, two or even three premises insecure during a week's tour of night duty. This too, added to the burden because it meant that time would be required to keep the premises under guard until the keyholder arrived.

There were occasions of course, when perhaps due to the administration requirements of earlier arrests, the second check of premises went amiss.

However, I say the following only to example the professionalism of officers in those days because I know that I was not the only one who, after being signed off duty, drifted around my beat on my own cycle (later vehicle) just to make sure that a door or window had not been obviously smashed in without me knowing about it.

As mentioned previously, this was a practice which reflected the fact that beat officers 'owned' their beats and in effect, felt responsible for anything happening on them. I doubt whether that sense of responsibility would apply today and if not, that would account for a huge change in the attitude of officers policing today and with it, the actual organisation and structure of policing.

In remote areas of a beat, it was not unusual to use various practices such as the placing of black cotton across wide entrances of say, industrial estates or shopping precincts, to indicate the passage of persons or vehicles and this, of course would, if it had not been disturbed, negate the need to make the second check. I only tried that a few times and often wondered what would have been made of this 'cotton trap' if it was not removed. For obvious reasons, that would not be frequently, if at all, though it would not take much to dislodge it because at some places it would just be held in place by a small piece of soggy chewing gum.

There was indeed, a method in our madness for us with wives or partners at home because having snuggled into some 'hot bum' and then drifting into a deep sleep after a night duty, had a premises been so damaged or burgled without it being noticed, you could guarantee that you would be woken by someone from the early shift who, on behalf of their supervisors or the CID would want to know what time that window or door was last checked. Being woken on nights by the day shifts was not that infrequent and the same sort of procedure would be adopted with unfinished jobs allocated during one's shift. If the message pad had not been endorsed with the action taken or with 'No Further Action' necessary – usually 'NFA', then the early turn sergeants would want to know why, so that they could ensure that someone had attended and at least, placated the complainant.

Now I know that times have changed and that there will never be enough police officers to match the demand of work being received but that has always been the case. I also know that in my day, the problems emanating from illegal drugs use and the dealing in them, was nowhere near what it is today; neither was cyber fraud. It was alcoholism that was the main cause of criminality and although drink related problems exist today, many of those have been replaced by drug related issues.

So, it matters not whether one policed in those older days or in today's environment with all its changes, the management of the officers under the control of their supervisors is paramount in ensuring the provision of a reliable police service. So far as 'on the ground' policing is concerned, the important cog in the wheel was the sergeants who ruled the roost. They were not exactly feared but you knew what to expect if you tried to take advantage. They were very much your bosses, and they possessed the knowledge and supervisory skills sufficient for purpose. Yet, they received little or no training, it was something that came naturally, and I suppose, they were the type referred to as 'born leaders. It was in my later years that I realised that they, or most were then sadly missing.

It was as the cog turned that all of a sudden, 'Leadership' and 'Man management' courses were introduced. Yes, I have included the 'MAN' bit as that was what they were called. It was from what I observed when conducting my reviews as a 'Retained Experienced Personnel, that I discovered that this management skill was lacking. Much of the team spirit and camaraderie remained but the respect of supervisors had now diminished and with an air of laxity. Christian names of supervisors were being used and apart from three stipes being on display, it was difficult to distinguish who was supervising who on the shifts.

Although we now live in vastly different times with a more relaxed and liberal outlook on life and society, I can be sure that whilst those supervisors of the past did not suffer fools gladly, the level of camaraderie and team spirit was at a very acceptable and indeed, enjoyable height. The team spirit on shifts and the tricks played on each other delivered us a state of enjoyment. I could write another book at what we used to get up to whilst ensuring the sergeant never caught us.

No police service with the thousands of officers enrolled and attested into them in the past, present or future will prevent undesirables from slipping through the vetting process. Indeed, we did have the odd idiot and I recall one being caught for 'nicker nicking' (stealing knickers off washing lines) and others being discharged as 'Peeping Toms' etc. I also recall others sacked for stealing in various forms. A case which I clearly recall involved a 'High School' lad from Hereford who joined a few years before me. I knew this chap as he grew up not far from where I lived, and we had both worked at Ledbury but not at the same time. He allegedly set up his own assault by handcuffing himself to some railings, denting his helmet and throwing it into some nearby bushes. He had lain where he was found for some time but whether by accident or design, the place where this occurred, was where he was bound to have been discovered if not by the public, by the early shift en route to the police station. Why he wanted to bring attention to himself in this way, (if that were the case) heaven knows but although it was never divulged exactly what had happened, he was suddenly out of the job in super quick time.

Returning to the present, what a sad day it was when Sarah Everard was abducted, raped, and murdered on 3rd March 2021 by the rogue Met. cop Wayne Couzens. How on earth could such a man escape notice within the ranks of his police force? This was the question posed to me by many of my friends and contacts at the time and initially, I hopelessly tried to defend the situation by saying that even with the strict vetting procedures I had experienced in the past, one could not always guarantee that one would not slip through the net. I argued that these people evolved and might not have necessarily possessed such characteristics when they were recruited. However, as time progressed, we learned that there were tell-tale signs which were completely overlooked. There was sufficient evidence to satisfy me, at any rate, that he should have been ejected much earlier before committing such atrocious crimes. But would that have stopped him? Probably not, but at least he would not have been able to pose as a police officer and his vile actions would not have besmirched the entire reputation of the police service to make us appear inept.

It seemed like only a short time afterwards, on 16th January 2023 that the news of yet another Metropolitan police officer, David Carrick had pleaded guilty to 49 offences of a sexual nature, many of them rape, which he had committed over a period of two decades whilst serving as a member of the Westminster and Diplomatic Protection Core. It beggars' belief and this will again dent the public's confidence and particularly their respect once held in their police. Another own goal and a huge leap backwards.

It was following the Sarah Everard murder that the Home Secretary commissioned Her Majesty's Inspectorate of Constabulary, (HMIC now merged with the Fire and Rescue service Inspectorate) to review the vetting procedures in operation by our current forces and to this end, on 2nd November 2022, two months prior to this latest David Carrick affair, that Mr Matt Parr CB presented his report – 'An Inspection of Vetting, Misconduct and Misogyny in the Police Service'. No doubt the vetting procedures I had endured when joining the police service were not so deep as I had later encountered when I faced the 'positive vetting' procedures at a time when I was first seconded to the HMIC myself. Every area of my life was then examined – banking, friendships, the social and sporting scenes I was involved in, even my sexual orientations were involved in the conversations held when the vetting officer spoke to my mates, and these were not confined to my police colleagues. But ironically, even then I had not been 'cleared' of the vetting procedure until I had already worked for six months (25%) of my two-year secondment.

I was also very surprised that no sooner after I had retired as a serving chief superintendent, I needed to be vetted again so that I could play a part in the 'Retired Experienced Personnel Scheme' (REPS). God! I had just retired with an 'Excellent Conduct' certification by my Chief Constable David Blakey. I was convinced that some young 'spotty' clerk in the HQ Personnel Department had overlooked that I was a retiring Chief Super and so, I had assumed that they would be going through the motions of my vetting which would be rubber stamped. In any event, who was I to question whatever motive was involved? So, I did not and although it never crossed my mind, I would have been confident that such vigorous vetting procedures would have remained. However, the HMI's report was earth shattering and makes it plainly obvious that not only have standards been allowed to drop, but most of them had been thrown out of the window. I could not believe that some police officers had been allowed to remain in office despite them having committed quite serious crimes. That would never have happened in my day.

With every force vetting procedure being closely scrutinised, it transpired that about one in five applicants should never have been accepted. Mr Martin Hewitt QPM joined the Kent Constabulary and is now a member of the Metropolitan force and more importantly, is the chair of the 'National Police Chiefs Council'. On the same day as Mr Parr's report was published, he appeared on national television to assure all viewers that every police force was now examining their pending disciplinary investigations concerning allegations of sexual and misogynistic allegations. He agreed that such events have adversely affected the publics image and perception of the behaviour of the police who are employed to protect society. However, he emphasised that most police officers live up to the highest esteem expected of the police, though work has to be done to 'Call Out' the remaining adverse culture existing. He also said that the failure of action to be taken following previous reports of this nature would not be allowed to happen again. Sloppiness makes us look so inept when we score such 'Own Goals'!

I cannot believe that our beloved police forces have allowed this situation to deteriorate to such a low level. In Mr Parr's words, "we have made it too easy for wrong people to join the police". He said that of 725 cases where vetting took place, there were 131 cases where the decision to employ was questionable. This process was not being taken seriously enough and some forces had not realised how important it is. It has become far too easy for the wrong people to get in.

By the way, I happen to wonder whether the reduction of 20,000 police officers ordered by Prime Minister Theresa May, may have influenced this situation. Most of those who left were seasoned officers who had been properly vetted. This perverse decision meant that the wheel had to be put back on and in the ensuing rush to recruit, I asked myself whether the vetting procedures involved were processed too quickly by employing short cuts to fill that gap – I don't know but I just wonder?

The report also identifies many instances concerning the monitoring of anti-corruption risks by officers. Whilst in my day, a business interest could not be maintained, neither could gifts or hospitality be accepted. Of course, there were ways around this including sheer non-compliance but since those days, Police Regulation amendments have been made approving such activities but where that occurs, registers must be kept, and close supervision given. It is the latter supervision which has apparently not been provided and has been identified as often the cause of the problem. Having skimmed through the report, the overwhelming conclusion I arrived at was that my old friend, 'Common Sense' had once again spun in his grave. The relaxation of the restrictions referred to above has merely opened the door for tighter measures to be applied despite the lack of them in the first place. The police force may not have been my chosen place to work in these days.

The practice of 'over legislating' will inevitably lead to an added bureaucratic existence which, although lending to a reduced level of supervision will negate the use of common sense. I could go on for ages about this, but I am sure those involved in the 'police family', will understand what I mean. It has been difficult for me to describe my 1960s policing world without dropping on some modern changes concerning methods and strategies. I am not that naïve to realise that the world does not stand still and as that solicitor friend of mine states "Evolution by its very definition, means change". However, as society or any process within our society evolves, one expects the resultant changes to equate to improvements. What bugs me, therefore, is that I cannot put my finger on any improvements in either our society or even with improved scientific advances aside, of the police service policing it.

So, with the realisation that our old ways were required to change with changing times, let me first continue with the varying subjects of yesterday, if only to acquaint the reader with the available benchmarks which were in existence from which guiding hands were used to make the changes. I am certainly not advocating that we return to those processes but in describing what took place to replace them, we are equipped to make up our own minds to judge whether those processes resulted in advances or whether along the path of progression or evolution, we have lost our way; in which case, glancing behind us might not be a bad idea after all.

So, even just for interest's sake, let us examine where we came from: -

10. Visibility and Communications

It was those nominal indices that I am working on in that above photograph many chapters ago, that reminds me that the only method of internally communicating with other police stations or other agencies, was by way of the post or telephone. In addition, county forces introduced their own internal delivery system through a few vehicles driven by civilian support staff. At West Mercia, force post would be received in the registry office at headquarters and sorted into a battery of baskets for delivery to the various offices in that building. In addition, that for despatching to other police stations would be collected by the divisional drivers for delivery to the police stations within their respective divisions.

So, in the field of crime prevention and detection, how did our police forces manage to impart essential criminal intelligence and other important information among us? On a national basis, how were the descriptions of wanted or suspected hardened criminals circulated from force to force or to the public? In cases of very heinous crimes, such details would of course, be advised to the public by use of the media of the day - commercial radio, television, and newspapers. Without large standalone computers and the telex system of messaging which came upon the scene many years later, much reliance was placed on Scotland Yard's publication called the 'Police Gazette'.

This was a publication first issued in 1772 by the chief Bow Street magistrate. It had been known as the 'Hue and Cry'. Having been re-named the 'Police Gazette', responsibility for its publication was transferred to the Metropolitan Police ('Scotland Yard') in 1883. The National Police Improvement Agency has since transferred those responsibilities, with the College of Policing. I could dwell on the historical perspective of the Police Gazette, but perhaps at another time.

I have always remembered how proud our little rural force was at the number of travelling criminals who were captured in Herefordshire because of checks being made of them against those indexed cards to the Police Gazette I was working on in that above photograph. It was a boring job to keep them accurately updated, I suppose that was why us cadets were used to do it. However, there was something of an aura about that system which somehow, ensured that the job would not be done otherwise than with accurate rigidity.

In addition, we were plagued by travelling criminals using hotels to 'stop over' without paying. Booking through electronic means and the use of bank cards these days has largely done away with those types of frauds but back then, it would not be unusual to walk into a hotel to book yourself in for that night or sometimes longer, then disappear without paying. Such offences were often committed by conmen who took on false guises such as vicars, airplane pilots etc. They had bags of **confidence** to play these parts and hence the name – conman evolved. To combat such scams, these regular fraudsters were made known in the Police Gazette and it was the duty of the aide to CID; the most junior detective, to transfer their details, including all their known aliases, into the 'hotel book'. The city hotels in Hereford would then be visited with the book to see if any of 'our friends' had booked in.

Although I cannot recall any successes with the hotel book, I often heard others bragging that "There is not many who could travel through Herefordshire without being caught." Such comments were more than likely proffered by members of the Traffic Department who, although only patrolled in about three high speed patrol cars at a time, (One per Division and later an additional one on the M50 Motorway) were good at stopping and checking the vehicles and their occupants at all times of the day or night.

Friendly competition existed as to who were 'Kings of the cops' when it came to positive stop and checks. I recall PCs Chalkie White and Brian Williams often vying with their colleagues Pete Knight and Charlie Day for this accolade on the Traffic Department'. Yes, that was the 'KNIGHT AND DAY' car!

The point I make is that these successes often resulted from a 'good nose' or a 'gut reaction'. It was called good coppering. It was required because of the keenness and competition to arrest more than their colleagues either individually or on shifts and so far as detection rates were concerned, on divisions. It makes me smile with frustration now, when I learn of the hullabaloo created over the so-called injustices of routine stopping and checking persons. I am especially annoyed that the 'black card' is often used to allege racism when such checks are made in areas predominantly occupied by black people. A level of racism might well have been applied on occasions, but why do not these critics realise that it is often those black persons, that are committing the crimes? There have always been crime areas which were not so heavily populated by non-white people but stopping and checking white people would have been carried out with equal vigour. I am guessing that nobody dare complain or point these issues out because they would get blasted with being racist and just cower down so as not to be controversial.

Stopping and checking was a practice which, with a neighbouring panda car driver, I often applied on night duty. We met up at a suitable location on the outskirts of Hereford on the main A49 road. I cannot ever recall stopping a black person. I agree they were not many of them in Herefordshire but the point I am making is that stopping and checking was a very good police tactic and not at all motivated by racism. This practise was synonymous with fishing as we did it on the basis that there were few others out and about in the middle of the night other than criminals and police officers. Just like fishing, we often had a good catch and on other expeditions, the bait was not so attractive. I doubt whether we would have made any stop checks at all if we were then, required to complete the administration required after each stop as they do nowadays. "Why Bother"? is the cry I hear nowadays.

We earned such a buzz after making a good check and it became a challenge between 'Them and Us.' With so few visible signs of the police in any hour of the day, it now often passes through my mind as to the number of criminals who now evade capture because they can travel around more easily without the fear of being stopped.

I suspect that automatic number plate recognition (ANPR) may have had an affect but even so, this will have seriously diminished the benefits derived from being able to 'communicate' (chat up) people at times which often led to surprise finds in their vehicles, including the occupants themselves. Of course, prior to our panda car days, we were more likely to perform such checks when on foot and in a position to challenge actions or the general behaviour of people who were also on foot. But here again, how often are police officers seen on foot patrol these days? This situation has developed into a massive dearth of communications between the police and the communities of today who they are supposed to serve. Not only does this reduce the chances of detecting and preventing crime, it causes the widening of the gulf between the police and the public to be dragged even further apart.

So that would be another area where our police are not now so often visible on the streets. With differences of case load to police officer ratios, I can accept that today, they probably have not got the time, but they have better resources and I am absolutely sure they do not have the same level of motivation. Those phrases I have heard, "What's the Point"? and "Why should we bother"? are sure indicators that morale among them and the camaraderie which had existed in times past, have now taken steep dives. If relationships are ever going to improve, morale and the camaraderie of police officers should be the first entity to be restored.

The other negative dive concerns the degree of time spent between the police and the community which hitherto, was fostered by that 'doughnut' structure I mentioned on pages past. This has resulted in the respect once held for the police by the community, now being replaced by a breed of our society who are more inclined to resist and question why we should be working in that way. No doubt with the additional freedom to police in those days, such powers were likely to have been abused in a minority of cases but that being so, resistance to being spoken to by the police seems to me, to have increased and caused so much hassle which is now often televised almost daily. Surely these programs do nothing but advertise to youngsters that the police are there to be abused and not to protect them?

And so, returning to those card indices in which that photograph portrays me at work, the introduction of the Police National Computer (PNC) in the early 1970s, proved extremely beneficial. All the information on those cards and very much more will be stored on it. What a great tool that would have been in my day, especially when considering the fact that similar data from all forty-three forces are now resting on that same database.

With the suspicions surrounding computers prevalent in those early days, I bet all those cards were kept for as long as possible 'just in case' but then reluctantly destroyed. But alas, communications were now being changed to electronic means and so unwittingly, our skills at talking to people were at the same time, being eroded.

And so, in the context of the question, "Where have all our police gone"? At that time, I bet that no-one gave an atom of a thought that it would then help to erode the art of stopping and speaking to people in order to use and hone their skill to sometimes persuade them to open the boot or provide personal details etc. Prior to and during those days, the expertise of talking to people to extract vital information from them often led to arrests, sometimes on a wing and a prayer from a mere 'gut reaction.'

As stated earlier, I can remember being told on my initial training that: - "If you think a person deserves to be arrested, then you will always be supported in that belief." That served me well in all those years when I came upon such situations.

Without the PNC, the ownership of vehicles was not readily available after office hours without hauling some poor civil servant from his bed to check the vehicles at the local taxation offices where they worked. Even then, there was always the chance that the vehicle had been sold on and was registered in a different county, but that documents had not been updated.

In addition to the Police Gazette, regional publications were similarly circulated, and their contents dealt with in the same way. It was the 'Midland Criminal Record Office' in Birmingham who were responsible for this in our Midlands area. It was known by all as simply – 'MIDCRO'. It also ran their own card system, but which was expanded to include descriptive details such as tattoos being worn by those convicted or suspected.

At Halesowen in 1973 when working as a detective sergeant, I used this system to eventually convict a rapist of a particularly nasty violent rape. The offender had a distinctive tattoo spreading unusually from one side to the other of the back of a hand. He had stolen a car in which the abduction outside a night club in Birmingham was made by pretending to be a taxi.

So, with this being pre-computer age, but with the aid of MIDCRO's 'hole punch' card system, a metaphoric needle was threaded through thousands of holes in cards which signified those with convictions for: - 1. Sexual Offences, 2. Motor vehicle thefts or 'taking them without consent' and finally, 3. Those with tattoos on the back of hands.

It would have been that much easier these days with PNC but Midcro's system produced three cards, one of which was our offender. He had a very good alibi which was supported by his family who firmly and genuinely believed that he had been in bed all night but, unbeknown to them, he had escaped from a bedroom where his brother was fast asleep to steal a car, pose as a taxi driver outside a night club, picked up two girls and after dropping the first, drove to an isolated spot where he raped the second girl. He then returned to that bed without anyone realising that he had left the house. This was an excellent clear up and earned me and other officers commendations but I include it here as an example of how primitive our aids were in those days without the Police National Computer. I also include it because the trial judge commended the woman police officer who had recorded the statement of complaint. He said that the offender could almost be smelled as he read it. That police officer was a member of the specialist policewoman's department which will be relevant when reading chapter thirteen ahead on 'Our Fairer Sex'.

It does not need me to describe how much faster and more accurate functions can be handled with computer applications. However, I contend that as efficient as they can be, they can also be a distraction and a cause of information being overlooked. We had no personal radios when I first started on the beat at Ledbury and with only two on a shift alternating every two hours at manning the station, we were out alone but could never guarantee that we would not be visited by the sergeant. God help us if our sergeant discovered us where we should not have been. When on the beat, there were no methods of communicating with the station at Ledbury but at Hereford, there were police pillars and police boxes but only a few. On most beats, there were none. Blue lights would flash on them if we were wanted and if they were not within our view, we needed to rely on the public to tell us they were flashing. "Do not rush to answer that lad" I was told by an older bobby. "Let the bastards get exhausted fighting each other before we get there"! If the sergeant wanted a pre-planned meeting with us, particularly on nights, he would arrange for us to be at a particular location to make a 'meet'. If there was no police pillar, it would invariably be near a pub or telephone kiosk. There were plenty of forms to fill in for various occurrences but there were also four main registers which required entries as follows: -

1. **The General Occurrence Book (GOB):** This was where anything of common interest to all shifts would be noted including the order being given to wear shirt sleeves. Maybe a burst water pipe had been noted with water gushing from particular premises or a shop window would have suffered a cracked windowpane. These occurrences being noted so that new patrols were updated, and their discoveries were not duplicated. A second column would be used for noting any actions taken.

2. **The Process Book:** This would contain details of everyone reported for a summons. Every entry was given a unique reference number which would stay with it until it had been dealt with. If this entailed a motor vehicle, then details of it would also be recorded. I mention the latter because the first person I ever reported was for parking a car in a 'no waiting' area. I religiously recorded all particulars of the driver and vehicle in my pocketbook but had failed to include the registration number.

3. **The Stolen Motor Vehicle Book:** Unlike the above registers, these were individually issued and carried with our pocket notebooks and although a little thinner, were about the same size. They were specially designed so that car registration numbers were recorded in alphabetical order. If a suspect vehicle was seen, it facilitated turning quickly to the appropriate page to check if it had been reported stolen.

4. **The Vacant Premises Book:** As I write this, I must concede that it does not seem possible or practical even in my later days that prior to going on holiday or for other reasons, people living in the posher houses or other places which, due to their appearance, probably attracted the attention of housebreaking thieves, could report details of their premises being vacant. There were no

guarantees, but it was generally accepted that operational duties permitting, attempts would be made to pay a visit to these premises, normally on the night shift and at least once during the period vacated.

In addition to these registers, on a weekly basis, headquarters would circulate what was a one piece of paper information sheet called 'General Orders'. As the name suggests, this was really nothing as newsy as a newsletter: it contained orders and gave information as to the rare promotions that were made, the details of the 'postings' of recruits, retirements, deaths, new legislation, operational orders and the like. In later years, the paper used was printed in a yellow colour and it quickly earned its nickname, the 'Yellow Peril'. Also, every police station had a telephone message pad made of hardboard and contained a clip, the same as found in lever arch files on which these messages were attached in chronological order. It should be obvious that any important message received by telephone, should be made known to all officers about to patrol their beats. But it was time consuming for the 'Station Reserve' officers to have to type them out.

It is difficult to think now, how we managed to circulate information without computers. The first signs of a breakthrough towards modern technology, was when a system called 'telex' was installed at force and divisional headquarters. Operators were trained to type messages which produced a narrow tape of it consisting of numerous coded holes. The tape would feed itself into the machine to convert it back into a readable format wherever it was received.

So, the implementation of electronic communications has caused all the above equipment and registers to be made redundant. "Good riddance", do I hear you say? I would agree bar for one aspect and that is, all those machines and registers were visibly apparent by their presence at strategic places. Their computerised replacements requiring passwords and logging on or searching for the correct applications. Garbage In – Garbage Out – or 'GIGO' as I learned on an early computer course, brought with it their own problems of accessibility and reliability.

A good example of what was lost is best described by the now redundant 'Briefing Parades' as will be described in the below chapter.

11. Getting Informed

It made common sense that before walking out to our respective beats, we should be fully aware of the contents of all those registers and messages described above. With so much to be absorbed, we were required to report for duty a full fifteen minutes before our shifts officially began. We had no idea then that we were not being paid for these fifteen minutes. Our supervisors often demanding that those appearing late for their briefing, needed to remain at work at the end of the shift to make up for the lost time. Yes, this was more of a military / disciplined regime than it is nowadays. But we were visible on our beats and the job was being done properly.

I have told the story many times before of my colleague Jim Whent who, when challenged by the sergeant as to why he was invariably late for early turn, explained that he had one deaf ear and due to him turning over in his sleep, he often slept on his good ear which prevented him from hearing his alarm. Some wag had the idea of forging a memorandum addressed to him from the chief constable in which he was ordered to attend the police surgeon's practice for a hearing test. This would have been a critical order to receive because in those days, had it been confirmed by the doctor, the officer would be in danger of being medically retired without receiving a full pension. Jim was not late again!

It was years later, not too long before I retired in fact, that the Police Federation (the union for officers up to chief inspector rank) caused this fifteen-minute briefing practice to be stopped. Although I had only then realised that the fifteen minutes briefing time had been in effect, voluntarily performed, I was gutted to think that our professionalism could be compromised in that way. We would be sent to our beats without possessing the proper tools! I guess that the Federation thought that they could squeeze more money out of the coffers and into our pockets by being paid for it but that thought had backfired and it never happened until probably it was absorbed into future pay awards. But ever since, Police Officers have been deployed often without face-to-face instruction. If they had taken the time to brief themselves, that would have meant that their beats would have been void of the presence of the officers concerned and as an aside, they could not now be castigated for not reporting early enough to be briefed.

The registers described above would not be found in police stations today. Most of their contents would now be contained within various force computerised systems often coupled with many other applications such as 'command and control' and 'Force Intranet' systems and accessed by those who considered this necessary. The problem with that is that hard copy of such information is rarely produced and with it now being a paperless society, not all will take the trouble to log in and access it unless done prior to the commencement of a shift.

So, whilst technology plays an important part, the details of such vital information will not have been accessed other than during duty time. I fully realise that modern day technology is such that data can be delivered by screens and mapping systems. In addition, intelligence departments can provide a daily product, much like our collators did when the fifteen-minute briefing period was cast to the wind. But do officers consider that obtaining the information is worthwhile to them?

In answering that question, I cast the reader back to my earlier gripe about the loss of rural and estate policing. As mentioned in my 'doughnut' philosophy some chapters ago, those officers who were responsible for the happenings on their beats would regard themselves as having an ownership for their policing responsibilities. They would be protective as to what happened on their beats. They would regard crimes not being detected as being a black mark and consequently, would pull out all stops to detect them.

In addition, the not so quantifiable benefit of having a meeting prior to each shift cannot be overlooked when it comes to gauging the camaraderie or level of morale which is so important in these team' occupations. The shifts of police officers are teams just like sportspeople and they should have a 'huddle' and chat before being deployed. I do not know the answer to this but would a team of nurses and doctors on a hospital ward take over a shift without being updated verbally (in addition to patient notes)? I hopefully doubt it.

Now fast forward to what I have described as 'Fire Brigade Policing' where most policing is done from hubs or centres. By comparison, the ownership of those areas and the crimes committed on them would not resemble the degree possessed by our colleagues in those years gone by. So, I contend that it is reasonable to assume that not so much interest or effort is now expended in what goes on in the extra-large patrol areas in which they work. Since my retirement, I have often heard the expression, "It's not a vocation anymore, it's just a job"!

So, can we also assume an increase in unreported crime? I contend that not a fraction of the crimes being committed today are being reported as they used to be. Those which are, are usually reported for the sake of insurance claims. My blood boils when I hear politicians (and police chiefs) claiming a responsibility for lower crime rates. You only need to listen to voices of the community to learn that crimes and criminal intelligence go unreported because of the belief that communities suffer a reduced police interest in their areas or because previous failures to attend the incidents which they have reported or even to respond to messages left for them.

In addition, it seems that we cannot make contact with any public agency or corporation these days without having to wait an inordinate amount of time for the phone to be answered. On many occasions recently, 30 to 45 minutes has been experienced and that is not unusual. How frustrating is it when eventually it is answered, only to have to plough through many options on an answer phone before we get to speak to a human being? Then only to be told on occasions that we had selected the wrong option! How dare the police and politicians brag that they have reduced crime? Confidence in reporting anything, including crime has disappeared because nobody feels listened to, even if they can be heard.

I became a member of the 'Nextdoor' platform so that I could start a volunteers' scheme at the start of the Covid 19 pandemic. That system often provides warnings given by members about suspected scams and now that we have CCTV all over our neighbourhood, people post clips of strangers prowling around their cars in the middle of the night. I have often asked them if they had reported such things to the police and without fail, I have never had a positive response to that question which indicates to me that it is not only the police who have adopted the 'What's the point' attitude', because of it, it has now spread to victims! The reasons compounding this assumed loss of interest by the police have been brought to my attention by existing officers and some retiring later than myself and, in every case, it seems that the lack of time and resources are a main factor but there remains an attitude reflecting the constraints that have been put their way over the years regarding the measures which have made it so difficult to have offenders successfully prosecuted. We are back to the "What's the point" attitude again!

And so, we broach another area which has contributed to our police not being so visible today. The administrative work required following the arrests of, or the reporting of offenders, was properly managed by the patrol sergeant conducting the briefing. He would make himself aware of that commitment required by his shift members and then arrange a rota so that officers were afforded this time without denuding the patrol strength of the beats. Very often, constables would be expected to pay visits to neighbouring beats when their colleagues were tied up with this paperwork.

In later years, as a member of the 'Retained Experienced Personnel' scheme, when reviewing undetected crimes, I became aware that that procedure had long been forgotten when I discovered that every police officer on duty at the main Kidderminster Divisional Police Headquarters was inside the station at the same time. On one occasion a civilian desk officer was confronted with a member of the public who had arrested his own adult son for stealing thousands of pounds by continuously 'borrowing' his father's credit card to withdraw cash from his account. The father with his 'arrested' son was told to return to the police station in the morning because no police officers were available. The son absconded from the area but when that was later reported by the father, the police officer deployed to investigate the crime had forgotten to circulate the suspect as a wanted person. She also recorded the crime as the theft of the credit card value 14 pence ignoring the thousands of pounds the son had stolen. The son had later been arrested in another police area for something entirely unconnected but of course, no knowledge of the offence committed in Worcestershire was available. A sergeant had made comments on the crime file held within the computerised system but had not identified anything wrong. I recall saying to myself that this was truly an indication that we now had arrived at the time when the blind was leading the blind.

I merely include the brief details of that incident here to emphasise that such a malfunctioning process of chasing the paperwork had also led to a disappearing police force. The business of being tied down by this administration has indeed, been tackled by various methods in the past, and have failed.

The main plank of attack on it occurred in the mid-eighties when I had been secondment to the HMI's office. Forces including my own, had discovered that the Metropolitan Police had launched a scheme whereby almost all the compilation of arrest reports and reports for summons (bookings) would be completed by a team of individuals who had been identified as being good at compiling them. These teams were called 'Administration Support Units' (ASUs). The assigned ASU officers would of course, be experienced enough to be aware of the evidence required and the necessity to have the stolen articles identified etc. Unless a subsequent 'Not Guilty' plea had been entered, the arresting officer could forget all about the administration connected with his arrest and would no longer be interested in it. On the face of it, this appeared to be an excellent scheme but whilst working in other forces during my 'Pre-Inspections of them, I began to pick up some disquiet. Apart from a central 'hub' where the ASUs were housed, some forces used a team of specialist officers attached to it to complete the statements required.

It was quickly realised that the rest of the officers in that station were receiving no experience at all in obtaining the necessary evidence to support criminal charges and by the way, who would be equipped to replace those expert officers when they retired or otherwise ceased those duties? Views had been expressed that we had been unwittingly building a two-tier policing system, one of them were just uniform carriers and the others became expert evidence gatherers. I am sure the problem was not that severe but on the face of it, we were building this team of warrant card holders who were mainly carrying out administrative duties.

12. The Civilianisation of Police Officers

Despite in whichever era I have policed in, ever since I can remember, there has always existed the problem surrounding the effectiveness of policing with insufficient resources. In the earlier days, recruits could not be attracted to doing the job as the pay and conditions were not attractive enough. In addition, the Home Office were usually reluctant to grant forces permission to increase the establishment of officers apportioned to them.

So, ever since panda cars were introduced circa 1967, the public and politicians have been crying out loud about the need to "put our bobbies back on the beat". 'Law and Order' was a very hot subject, particular with politicians around election time. It was not surprising therefore, that particularly around the turn of 1985, the Association of Chief Police Officers (ACPO – now the National Police Chief Council -NPCC) were urged to find more bobbies to put back on the beat from those who were judged as being employed on duties which did not require the carrying of a police warrant card. This policy was of course, very attractive to the government and local authorities who saw it as partially satisfying the demand through cheaper means. I recall a concerted effort to apply such a policy between 1985 to 1987 when I was employed as staff officer to Sir John Woodcock, one of Her Majesties' Inspectors of Constabulary (HMIC). However, whilst there were many examples of these jobs ripe for civilianisation, many were being performed by officers who otherwise, because of some sickness or injury, were precluded from performing street duties. We were so sympathetic to those types of cases because the only alternative for them was to be retired on a medical pension and that did not gain any benefit to anyone other than freeing up the authorised numbers on the police establishments which mostly could not be filled in the first place.

There was one other exception which will always be remembered by me. Sir John Woodcock observed, **"If anyone feels it necessary to visit a police station**

for whatever reason, he or she will be wanting to speak to a police officer, not a civilian who will not have had a police officer's experience".

I fully agreed with that sentiment but of course, as time marched on, so far as I am aware, all police front counter clerks in police stations became civilian support staff. The argument made by Sir John had fallen on deaf ears. In addition, many police stations have now been closed so whether by personal visits or by telephone or electronic means, it is now highly likely that the first contact with the police will be with a member of police support staff.

Sir John would not have been happy. The example I gave in the last chapter concerning the father arresting his son for stealing many thousands of pounds from him by repeatedly 'borrowing' his credit card, is an excellent example of what can go wrong. I have no doubt that had one of the police 'Station Reserve' officers of yesteryear, been behind that desk, one of those officers on the shift who at that time, were all inside the police station, would have been released from their paperwork and directed to deal with the situation efficiently.

It had also not been taken into consideration that those police officers working at the front counter desks were generally regarded as possessing a high degree of police professionalism. They expected the job to be done by all their colleagues on their shift, which included their fellow patrol sergeants, to a high level of efficiency. They were also, generally located very near to the control rooms and when desired, often directed which officers should attend the various incidents being reported. Their status as experienced and efficient police officers were such that at some forces, this kudos was signified by allowing them to display an added crown just above the sergeant's chevrons on the sleeves of their uniforms. They were not paid any more than their colleague sergeants but by golly, that kudos meant a great deal to them. Even in the poorer forces such as in Herefordshire, where these duties were performed by constables known as 'Station Reserve Officers' it was those constables who ran the show in the police stations and generally commanded deployments when radios were later introduced. Whatever their rank, they could put so many things to bed just with a kindly word or two of advice which in most cases, was all those callers to police stations required. They could also eject them out of the police station when they were there to cause trouble. So, when these officers began to become 'civilianised' they were replaced by well-meaning people who had not a clue about any aspect of policing or the law. Some were retired police officers but by and large, they more than likely were totally inexperienced and completely ill-equipped to do that job. It therefore took a very long time for them to build up enough knowledge and confidence to be able to deal with the public's problems but even now, although they are far more competent, there will be occasions when a police officer is required to provide advice.

But civilianisation still does not negate the dissatisfaction of those who took the effort to call at a police station to see a police officer. But of course, many, if not most, would use the telephone or electronic means to make enquiries or report their problems. We know this when we watch those 'fly on the wall' documentaries on TV. Very often, the full telephone conversations are actually heard, and the caller will be answered by a civilian controller as opposed to a police officer. Even in my time as a force operations room inspector in 1974, the shifts answering 999 emergency calls comprised a peppering of constables who were unable to perform outside duties, but the majority were civilian personnel. In the main, they all developed into excellent controllers but without a thorough grounding in police work. The HMIs were of course, at least being seen to obey the demands of the Home Office and indeed, the percentage of police posts which were eventually civilianised in every force slowly began to grow.

I was not, of course allowed to be involved in the inspection of my own force, but I never celebrated the fact that at one time, the percentage of civilianisation in West Mercia reached 50% of the police establishment and was the highest in the region. It was my personal view that West Mercia had overcooked the goose given to the police service by the Home Office whose only objective with this policy was to reduce the expenditure of employing police officers and at the same time, increasing their visible number on the beat.

Counter clerks, controllers and despatchers were not of course, the only positions which were replaced due to civilianisation. It was always the case that each divisional clerk held the rank of chief inspector. The savings involved at that rank were obviously attractive and over ensuing years, they were replaced by civilian personnel. Those then employed in that capacity, were paid a good salary but they would in effect, be the police and civilian personnel officers for their divisions and they would run the devolved budgets concerning the financing of it. They were just about in control of everything other than policing and in my case, as a divisional commander, I recognised them as a very important personal assistant or dare I say it – 'Right hand man'. Yes, I can say it because indeed, on the retirement of a male divisional clerk in my Redditch Division, I employed a lady to succeed him from many good applicants and a fine job she did as my right-hand lady.

Other former police jobs coming immediately to mind which were civilianised included coroner's officers, property officers, warrant officers, driving instructors, IT and communications department personnel, administration and 'pay' personnel and many more which now escapes my memory. My own opinion is that overall, these civilianised positions would have freed up many police officers, having the effect on increasing the visibility of officers on patrol who made up the establishment of regular officers. However, I would not have civilianised any position which involved the first contact with members of the public. As my old boss implied, anyone who contacts the police would expect a police officer to respond to them. Also, the policy of employing those experienced officers suffering with medical conditions which precluded them from normal policework was an excellent idea and should have remained. In addition, where that is not possible, all civilian personnel so employed should be closely supervised to ensure that tragedies such as that described in chapter three, when Janbaz Tarin stabbed to death his estranged wife and her mother are prevented or minimised. That is not to indicate that that was the problem because I simply do not know if that was so.

13. Keeping Up Appearances

The briefing parades described at chapter eleven were steeped in tradition but in any event, they were also beneficial to our supervisors who could check us out to ensure that we were smart enough to patrol our beats. Many of those old sergeants briefing us had completed their national service and some had returned from the war. We were therefore deployed by them, much like a military squad, all stood in a row dressed as smart as we could with our helmets on and boots 'bulled' military fashion. We each held our truncheon, handcuffs, whistle, and pocketbooks on display. These collectively were referred to as our 'appointments' but heaven knows why.

The way we presented ourselves was very important and comment would be made by the sergeant if trousers were not properly creased and boots shining. Infrequently, officers were sent home to smarten themselves up and sometimes this meant, to have a shave. They worked overtime at the end of the shift to make up for the lost time they had incurred. Our uniform dress was strictly supervised to such an extent that we would never be found in public without our helmets unless they had been accidentally dislodged, perhaps during scuffles on the ground. Shirt sleeve order would only be given by the head of each sub-division and when this was allowed, everyone was required to comply with it. Officers were not allowed to be in 'shirt sleeve order' without such an order being given by the divisional commander.

Our appearance, however, was not always on public display. We naturally had those spots where we could shelter from the elements and be treated to warm drinks in winter and cool ones in summer. Often, and not within public gaze, these were accessed through the back doors into cafes, restaurants and the bakeries were always a good bet to get a drink and a warmup in winter. We were strictly off our beats, but it was amazing how information was picked up merely by having a chat with those working in these places.

Shopping or eating in public would not even have been thought of and my heart now sinks when I see officers emerging from shops or filling stations eating their chocolate bar purchases, often without wearing their headgear and sometimes returning to their police vehicles which had been parked inappropriately. It is so sad that we have now allowed our officers' appearances to drop below anything which would have been acceptable in years gone by. Seeing a police officer in public is a rarity but then when I do, they often look such a mess especially when they have chosen not to wear their headdress.

I know they now have so much more to carry or append from their bodies, but they are no longer upright looking officials who just by their stature and appearance, automatically demanding respect. Once, to be recruited, men were required to stand five feet ten inches tall and women five feet three inches. But of course, sex discrimination decreed that this was not fair. Instead of being a specialist policewomen's department, some women wanted to do the same duties as their male counterparts. Sex discrimination through 'Equality' had raised its ugly head and of course, in allowing them to be similarly deployed, the height restrictions were lifted because it could not be fair for women to be allowed to join at 5' 3" when if a man, you were not allowed to join at 5' 9". It sounds stupid, doesn't it?

Of course, it seemed that no-one had the courage to question whether petite short women could do the same job, which was why there had been a difference in the height restrictions in the first place. No-one bothered to ask why it was that men were barred from joining if they were below 5'10" but women could join at 5'3". To question that, would certainly not be politically correct. I had heard of the words sexism, prejudice, discrimination and of course, chauvinism but never misogyny which appeared to me, to be the same as those synonyms but which had been little used. Perhaps it had been dug up to suit this particular scenario?

So, we drifted into a world where, although many a short woman could do the job better than many of their taller male colleagues, generally speaking, ladies were not built to equal men in the many duties which required a male police presence. Forgive the puns but 'in short' they were 'by and large' simply not strong enough.

In addition, no-one will be able to persuade me that our police ladies will never be required to be 'backed up' by male officers but of course, there are occasions when police need backing up no matter what gender. However, the probability is that our female colleagues will require a little extra support. I have seen it on TV in 'fly on the wall' documentaries. I witnessed this change-over at first hand and concede that probably most women are happy with how they are now deployed. But that will only be because they have been recruited to that role, a role which they desired. But of course, with the loss of our specialised Policewomen's Departments, we have lost their expertise. They were used to harvesting the evidence from females and children in all types of sexual attacks and they were good at it. Complainants would far prefer to be seen by such officers than a 'hairy a***d' male officer.

So, I now occasionally groan when I see officers in their yellow 'Hi Viz' jackets. Since 1829, we had worn our very smart black tunics with those silver-coloured buttons gleaming down the front centre of them. Health and Safety has taken its toll. But come on, if it has been decreed necessary for the health and safety of officers to wear them, then why aren't we all wearing them whenever we venture outside our homes? I even saw a chief constable in front of TV cameras wearing one recently. It was of course, brand spanking new – creases and all but I suppose his thinking was that his officers were required to wear them then he should. Hmmm. Even if they are deemed necessary, and I will dispute that in any forum, why must they be the same colour as all the others, mainly our highways workforce and any other outside worker who takes a fancy to wear one. Also, if they are deemed to be necessary, why cannot the sleeves just contain such reflective material which would leave the rest of the tunics smartly presented to the public.

We have all failed to fully always concentrate on the road ahead at all times, so have you ever suddenly reacted when you see ahead, maybe a gaggle of people in yellow 'Hi Viz' attire? I bet your first reaction is to brake and check your speed – just in case; but then all you have seen are workmen doing whatever they are doing on the side of the road, often with the other 95% of them watching or supervising. (Sorry, must not get my grumpiness diverted into my other dislikes) The absence of police headdress for most probably, safety helmets might finally register as a good clue that they are not police officers. Yes, there were always heavily built rotund police officers in tunics but somehow, they did not look so bad as they do in often-dirty yellow plastic Hi-Viz jackets.

With our changing police objectives brought about by a sickening society where life has been deemed as being so cheap that knife attacks and firearms are increasingly used to stem life, one can imagine that our police must be equipped with the tools to do the job. Stab proof vests and on the other hand, collarless shirts and whatever else it takes to make the attack on such low-life easier to combat. But not all officers are required on these 'sharp end' duties. Baseball caps, black open necked shirts, creaseless trousers narrowed down into appropriate footwear seem to have become the norm to be worn by many officers who are more than likely never going to have to be on that front line. Can we ever get back to producing officers on the beat to be appropriately dressed to increase the respect they deserve? The 'Task Force' officers or whatever else they are called – Firearms response, even dog handlers should be appropriately dressed for their jobs but please let's get those on show on the beat – (when we see them), appropriately dressed to fly the flag as was once the case. That's such an easy discipline measure to reintroduce and it sad that we haven't got the leaders in situ to do it.

14. Our Fairer Sex

So having touched upon the appearance and stature of our lady officers above in the context of the discontinuance of height restrictions, this is probably the ideal place to continue that debate which for me, is by far the most 'delicate' of subjects I shall deal with. For that and the reasons appearing below, I do not mind adding that it will not be my favourite subject.

I had been fortunate enough to have witnessed the transformation of the policewomen's department from being 'specialist' officers who mostly dealt with females, children, missing persons, and anything else where it was felt that the soft touches of a female officer might be better served. But then, almost overnight, the introduction of equality legislation demanded that they be thrown into the pot of all police officers, and they became 'just' police officers themselves, doing whatever their male colleagues were challenged to do. Being fortunate to be among them when they were 'forced' to convert themselves, I'm aware that some would have enjoyed the metamorphosis, but I can also tell you that many, if not most, hated it and it didn't take them long to resign. I have spoken to two of those recently and they confirm how terrible that time was. They were always supervised by female sergeants and inspectors and in larger forces, Superintendents. Now they came under the command of the same supervisors as their male colleagues, and this meant that there was a great deal of bullying and sexism. Many of those that stayed later resigned but some enjoyed it and stayed until they drew pension.

Let me first declare where I stood then and where my beliefs are held today. I thought that this transformation of them was so utterly wrong. Apart from God or the process of evolution whichever you want to believe, my belief is that the opposite sex was primarily on this earth for reproduction purposes and yes, I was quite happy that with husbands or partners bringing in the bread, they were also the lead gender who were more suited to being the homemakers as well as mothers.

Stone age beliefs maybe, but so be it; I am more inclined to be chauvinistic but not sexist or misogynistic so far as that means the relegation of females to a lower order. I know full well that necessity will declare that our ladies may, at some periods be required to top up the household income. Also, that there are females in all kinds of vocations and callings, including to my knowledge, blacksmiths, bricklayers, heavy lorry drivers and the list goes on. We are now used to our ladies being involved in more sports than hitherto and God bless our female swimmers, rowers, football team, rugby team and our boxers all of whom and more, have brought home recent successes.

Yes, but those apart, surely the majority of us males certainly believe that they are better loved in their feminine form and pastimes. I cannot believe that there is anything wrong in my beliefs and I shall always treat women with probably more respect and courtesies than most of the males I come across.

I realise that in making that statement, I have openly declared that in that respect, I am a male chauvinist or sexist, homophobe, jingoist, or any other synonym likely to set me apart from what has turned into offending the principles of sex discrimination as we know it today. Just like the topics of human rights, I believe that those responsible for tweaking the balances have gone completely overboard and have used another sledgehammer to crack another nut.

But let me again quickly throw in to add to my stance, that I am not generally against our ladies being held in the highest of esteem if it means that they can compete with, and do all the things that males do, without using their gender as a tool to achieve those positions. Put another way, apart from organised mixed gender events, such as mixed golf, bowls, rowing and other specially organised mixed teams and events. On the other hand, I can see no reason at all why they should not be the head of any business, organisation or any other section of our human society, so long as they have been selected as possessing the best skills required for those positions. As an aside, I have recently joined a croquet club and that game is an ideal example where the ladies can tan the backsides of us chaps on any day of the week.

More importantly, I cannot see why ladies should not, in our more modern society, escape the shackles of being completely the homemakers alone. Why should they be totally responsible for waiting on us – "hand, foot and finger" as I have been told many times in the past! Yes, they are built to bear and suckle our young but so far as the mechanics of 'making home' are concerned, there is no reason why us men should not equally contribute and I shall not speak to anyone again who lets my wife know of what I have written here and if she discovers this, I shall not be doing the ironing again!!

I have obviously known many hundreds of policewomen during the time since 1960 when I first joined the constabulary. They were and are, of course, just like us males, of a vast mixture of types and characters. Even when they were members of their own department, they were of a mixed variety in every sense of the word. Some could throw a drunk out of a pub without blinking and some were of the more tender variety.

Of course, those separate boxes into which they were categorised, cannot exist today because they have all now, been recruited with their eyes wide open to the fact that they will carry out their duties as equals with both genders alike. Whilst fully understanding the fact that there are many women whose skills in every aspect are far superior to their male counterparts, I just cannot bring myself to believe that generally speaking, the female gender is as well suited or equipped to policing on an equal basis to their male counterparts. Equally, I cannot believe that the male 'copper' is as well suited to those jobs previously performed by policewomen when they were members of their own 'specialist' departments.

My next confession concerns the misogynism that existed in my time and to which I may have unwittingly contributed in jest, without fully realising the affects which might have resulted from those actions. Yes, much 'banter' was going on and yes, I can hear the uproar from those who believe that this 'banter' was used as an excuse for sexism. It was never intended to be from my part. Indeed, I have conducted some research with our policewomen of my time, and they concur that whilst some could give better repartee in defence, there were those supervisors among us (sergeants in the main) who they felt were bullying them. Indeed, one left the job on recommendation by her husband who was also a police officer.

As suggested above, there were also obviously some who treated this like water off a duck's back and could give as good as or more than they received. On the other hand, we went through a period, probably just before my retirement and which continued for some time afterwards, where some policewomen took to the civil courts, and some were awarded thousands of pounds for receiving such treatments having suffered mental turmoil causing them to leave their employment. I have no doubt that most of these cases were true, and I am supported in that belief due to the awards of compensation they received. On the other hand, I would be lying if I had not at least wondered what, in some cases, their main purpose of seeking retribution in the courts was. The fact that not all cases were proved possibly suggests that some were taking actions just for the money.

Were they suited to the job in the first place? It would not be beyond reasoning why others in that position had not just left their employment, just like my friend described above had. They had decided that the job was not for them and just found other jobs. One also wonders about the recruitment process in being at that time. Was it good enough to ensure that our recruits were suited to policework and all that it entailed?

I must say that the 'Diversity' course I had attended at Kidderminster Police Station on the 8th and 9th of May 2002, taught me a great deal. Mine was not the first of these courses, there were many completed long before I attended, and they continued for a long time afterwards. I have also discussed their content with other ex-colleagues more recently and although it was not on my particular course, I had been appraised by a friend that there were many who treated it as a joke. One story concerned an ex-detective constable who coincidentally, I had supervised when I worked as a Divisional DCI. The story goes that he was almost late attending and as he walked into the full classroom, he spotted a fellow detective policewoman. He acknowledged her **with "Hiya bitch! Get the kettle on and let's have a cuppa before we start this!"**

The DC in question was known to be a comedian and of course, there was no way that his request was a serious one; I am sure he was not motivated to offend and was trying to make a joke of the course; the laughter that followed proved the point, but of course, he was of course, completely out of order. When instructed to attend this course, my feelings were that it was completely inappropriate but having completed it, I could acknowledge that messages were received loud and clear and it left me with two main thoughts: -

1. Although I had taken part in that so called 'banter' with my female colleagues, I was very content in the knowledge that anything I had said to them, banter or otherwise, would not have been hurtful in any way. It would be wise however, not to partake in such behaviour again.
2. My conclusion at the end of the course was that what had been preached as the main 'plank' of the subject was correct, but just like my comments above regarding 'Human Rights and Equality', the subject had been really overplayed by us police when it got to the workplace. Yet again, I thought that the tweakers had over tweaked.

We had been told that we should not refer to our mates by their 'nicknames' even though we believed that these were terms they sometimes favoured. Yes, there may well have been some that secretly harboured their dislike of their nicknames but surely, in the majority of cases that would be overkill. However, we all have friends who may not have nicknames but are often referred to by an abbreviated version of their full Christian names. Most I know, refer to themselves this way – Chris, Dave, Gord, Jim etc. but of those I am not so familiar with, I have since made a habit of asking whether they prefer to be addressed by their Christian name in full or their abbreviated version. I was once told by a Stephen that his name was, indeed, Stephen and not Steve. That always reminds me. I have been playing golf with a certain Roger and I had witnessed some others in our group refer to him as Rog and others as Roger. And so, I asked him which he preferred, and I admired him for his diplomatic answer – "Most call me Roger" he said. What a diplomatic way of telling me that he did not favour 'Rog'. He is now Roger but even though I have sometimes slipped up – I have then immediately corrected myself with an apology.

We were also informed about a Police Dog handler who had been suspended from duty because he had referred to a Chinese 'Take Away' premises as a 'Chinky'. He had been tracking a burglar and was asked for his location by his sergeant controller – he responded, "We've just passed the 'Chinky' Sarge".

This was all very strange to me but the biggest shock I had concerned road traffic accidents which, since time immemorial were always abbreviated to RTAs. It was of course, the letter 'A' in that acronym that caused offence. It was the injured and those close to persons who were fatally killed in them who objected to them being called 'Accidents'. They argued that if these incidents were caused owing to some degree of blame, then how could they be referred to as accidents? From then on, they were referred to as 'Road Traffic Collisions'. Or RTCs. For goodness' sake, what is the world coming to and what in the world possesses those responsible for bowing to such pressure? Are not there any more pressing problems to put right – like catching criminals -albeit as they are yet to be convicted, perhaps we should always refer to them as suspects right up until the time of conviction?

Whilst I never used email prior to my retirement from the job, I have never since objected to the receipt of jokes from my friends, relatives and colleagues; indeed, I have compiled my own email group which I call my 'Jokers'. However,

I must also plead guilty to receiving some which, as an afterthought now, might well have offended some minority group, politicians, or the other sex. On the other hand, I did cause comment to be made to one such 'non police' contact who sent me something which I can only describe as obscene. I told him so and he apologised and has never sent me such images again. Indeed, I have not heard from him since!

I also occasionally continued to receive jokes which nowadays would not be acceptable but might well have been in years gone by. However, I constructed a self-made policy of not forwarding them on to members of my own 'Joker' group and thus they would be deleted. It is noticeable that the receipt of such media content has vastly declined over recent years and that must be a good thing.

So, in conclusion and in my view, whilst there exist women who believe that they can do the same job as their male counterparts in the police, I would be happy that they continue to be employed as such but would much prefer that they reverted to their former roles where their expertise was made far better use of and produced the results that we no longer experience. We have lost that expertise and miss it. I concede that probably most women are happy with how they are now deployed. But that will only be because they have been recruited to that role, a role they desired. But where now is the expertise, we lost when our 'Policewomen's Departments' were disbanded?

15. Where Have All Our Police Gone?

As may have been realised, or expected, I had originally planned to have written this book in two, even three separate parts in the chronological order of events – 'The Old School' and then the 'New School' and possibly the aftereffects as the 'Third Part'. However, I have discovered that whilst I have gone along with that strategy where appropriate, some topics are better presented by immediately countering those old practices of the past, with the modern changes made. I am therefore concerned that readers may have wondered why I have changed tack immediately within some topics, but not in others. In cases such as this problem of police visibility or the lack of it, there are sections where it has been appropriate to immediately present the modern-day equivalent, in addition to separately dealing with it in its entirety. If I have caused confusion, I apologise, so I shall progress with that strategy as and when I think appropriate to do so.

I mentioned much earlier that I would be returning to the effects of Unit Beat Policing at the appropriate time. This has been one subject which I have referred to over many others. I contend that this time had such a huge influence on the death of community policing. The appropriate time has been difficult to determine exactly but I guess that this juncture is as good as any, and I shall refer to it later in this chapter because its implementation has not only affected the organisation and structure, but it has also had a disastrous effect on the prevention of crime through the lack of the visibility of our patrolling police officers.

What I cannot get over these days are the many reports either featuring in the media or those I am verbally taken to task about, which concern the lack of police visibility and, or the lack of communications between the police and members of the community. They question today, "Where have all our police gone"? With 'Panda' and then 'Response cars' now in their minds, even long after I had retired, I am often begged to get the bobbies back on the beat where they can be seen. (As if I could!) In this vein, I am often embarrassed by colleagues and associates in the various clubs and organisations I belong to when I hear of police not being contactable physically or not even answering email or voicemails. I add that in both the latter cases, I too have also experienced this failure. They have also referred to the police not attending incidents of concern to themselves or others. Such attempts to contact the police by members of the community, had obviously been made in the belief that the reasons for attempting contact were serious enough to attempt that contact in the first place. I suspect that most will not try again unless in extreme urgencies. This just adds to the diminished confidence held in our police which for so little effort, has had such drastic consequences.

It would be very naïve of me to expect the organisation and structure of the police service to remain exactly how it was when I retired. It is hard to believe that there are now far more police employed than when I was involved but of course, I realise that times have changed. For a start, drugs abuse and cyber or 'online' crime will now have taken up a huge slice of police time. We were free of all that and it is consequently, that true comparisons cannot be properly made.

We always said that we were very good at re-inventing the wheel. In simplistic terms, it seemed that we were to suffer regular reviews of the organisation and structure of our forces. It would not have been so bad if those re-organisations were due to the changing trends and the duties performed as a result, but they were mostly concerned with environmental and geographical changes. On many occasions, some changing decisions of reviews had returned to the status quo. It wasn't only politicians that could perform 'U' turns!

It may have been coincidental, but it seemed that these reviews regularly appeared to be made following some change of senior command or a politically inspired review had been ordered. It was as if whoever was responsible wanted to leave their mark on the force to emphasise their importance. I nearly left the force earlier on retirement because it was the Sir Patrick Sheehy review that had decreed that my rank of chief superintendent and that of chief inspector were not necessary. Some were even paid bounties to leave, but I wanted to carry on and it was a good job that I did because it was soon discovered that we weren't to be cast aside as first thought? The communities we serve would probably never have felt the difference, but that did not matter because they would be unconcerned provided that their police could easily be contacted and were 'visible', whilst providing an effective and efficient policing service. We formed consultative committees and 'multi-agency' working parties – bodies I never hear of today. Maybe they still exist – I simply do not know but I do not see evidence of their existence in local newspapers or in the operation of police practices.

Of the changes that have occurred since my retirement, the one that has come as a tremendous shock to me and is a subject which I do not mind saying that I thought would never raise its head, concerns the number of police stations which have now been closed completely or which are not now open to the public on a 24/7 basis. The speed and widespread nature of these closures have really surprised me. Modern technology will be offered up as the reason, I'm sure but surely financial savings or the introduction of such electronic means of communications would not have been the core reason why these police stations have closed? Common sense dictates that more officers should be seen on patrol but of course, invariably, even if so, they will be deployed from more of a central 'hub' and in direct conflict with our police being 'community' based. That is tantamount to taking another giant step away from community policing. Far cheaper of course, but not helping to remove that 'Fire Brigade Policing' tag. It's no wonder some have moved into fire brigade premises!

Many chief constables are now preaching that they are putting every effort into regaining the confidence in the police by returning to 'Community Policing'. Is that hypocritical or what, when on the other hand, they are closing police stations? If they think that community policing is driving around in a car, then they are very mistaken. But with no premises to police the community from, how will those officers manage without hiring premises? Some of the Police Stations where I have previously worked with 24 hours around the clock shifts and an enquiry desk have now shut down or have had their enquiry desk facilities either discontinued or reduced with telephone numbers available to ring in urgent cases. Many now operate in mobile facilities which is fine if they are in locations not previously operated from. Also, many now share facilities with the fire brigade or with other partners, some in less than convenient places. The West Mercia PCC John Campion states: -

"West Mercia is a safe place, where crime is relatively low. However, too many people do not feel safe and that is something I remain committed to changing. We have heard loud and clear from our communities what they want, and that is a visible and accessible police force. They also want to know that their concerns are being listened to and acted on. I will therefore continue to focus West Mercia Police on ensuring they are visible and accessible in the communities they are policing, focused on fighting crime and addressing the priorities of that community".

West Mercia and most other forces will have been encouraged to perform reviews or estate strategies. Inevitably this will be budget led and inevitably I would wager that despite objectives being set, it will not increase the visibility of the police. Indeed, those actions may well have driven visibility and communications with the police further away from community policing than ever. Never would I have dreamed in a thousand years that police stations in fairly large towns which had previously supplied local policing on a 24/7 basis would cease to become manned police stations with a front desk open to the public at all times.

Neither the Commissioner or the Chief Constable Pippa Mills who commenced her police service two years after I retired, have worked under a real community police system and would not be able to easily identify one, though Pippa Mills whilst serving in Essex had committed herself to form a modern-day process akin to it. The justification that electric communications have replaced the need will simply not wash with me. It certainly would have affected the degree of use but people who call at police stations really wanted to discuss something or else they would have used other electronic means. However, one has only to attempt to contact a police station by telephone, that is if the number can be found, when they invariably will be greeted by an automatic message. Messages left and often emails are simply not always responded to. I tried to set up an interview with one who, our village newsletter stated was responsible for the village area where I lived. This concerned my research for a previous book I was writing. I had never seen this police officer in the village, and I later learned from him that his responsibilities extended far from just our village. I had failed at three attempts to even get a reply from a voicemail I had left. This resulted in me enrolling the help of a CPSO at a clinic from where it was advertised that she operated in a town centre library. It was this CPSO who made me aware that the town's police station was no longer offering a front counter service for enquiries to be made. Indeed, it was shut but a telephone number was available. She promised to make the police officer aware of my desire to speak to him. He eventually knocked on my door weeks after the book had been published. I learned that most 'policing' activity is now performed by a handful of officers and a gaggle of Police Community Support Officers (CPSOs). Undoubtedly, it appears that these CPSOs are holding the 'Police' flag for most things these days.

Despite my early resistance to their formation being based on the likelihood that they would be turned into cheap police officers, they were so employed and are now very much more visible on the streets than police officers. From what I have seen, they are doing an excellent job but yes, they are performing low level work once performed by police officers. They are also inevitably being dragged into police stations to use information technology to spread the word. I receive almost daily a newsletter informing me of crime prevention advice, the latest scams and recent crime activity and appeals for assistance. The surgeries that they occasionally hold are very good but they are always organised and manned by CPSOs, and police officers cannot normally be seen. I hope that this publication will at least throw some light on how, over the years, our police visibility has steadily deteriorated, and why.

My experience has led me to wonder whether their powers and duties could be further expanded to perform community police duties as it was originally recognised. Letting them take the oath and with additional training and police uniforms, that would be the first positive step to retake community policing, and it would not cost a fortune and I'm sure the concept would fall in line with what maybe in present discussion at the Home Office. Such a 'two tier' police service which is visible, will now be a stride forward in bringing policing back to the communities and in any event, would be far superior to what we experience these days.

So, as a complete 'U' turn from the strategy I described at the commencement of this chapter, I need to make comment about the policing effectiveness prior to and following the days of those constabulary amalgamations and then the introduction of our new 'Panda Car' policing. Having policed at the sharp end of both eras, I can only say that to me, the effectiveness and efficiency did not appear to have changed one iota and did not attract a great deal of negative comment AT THAT TIME. The changes had just begun and had not then fully bitten. Hardly any affects were felt by the Borough and City Forces that escaped being amalgamated because they could cope with their smaller boundaries and inflated numbers of personnel. In the counties, the doughnut method as described above ensured that every inch of a police forces land was police supervised. Members of both types of forces were not complaining but more to the issue, neither were the communities they served. However, as the work to staff ratio increased, so did 'short cut' measures and a heavier reliance was required to be placed on the use of police vehicles which earned the tag, 'Fire Brigade Policing'.

There was still unrest concerning the ability of chief officers to post 'county' officers anywhere within the boundaries of their forces, many of the officers were fed up with being posted from pillar to post all over a county, but nothing could be done about it because living in one's own house would not, in any event, stop chief officers from dictating where you lived. So obviously, although in some forces where this was permitted, not many took up that option. In any event, police authorities were loathed to move those officers because of course, their removal expenses would need reimbursing.

Unit Beat Policing (UBP)

So, by roughly comparing methods of years past with the new era, we finally arrive at the post-mortem report concerning the death of 'Community Policing'. In my view, The beat bobby has always represented the root of community policing as was indeed, the idea behind Sir Robert Peel's thinking when, in 1829 he planted the seed of London's police. It is also my view now, that it was the introduction of Unit Beat Policing in the mid-1960s, which, albeit in hindsight, was the start of the destruction of Community Policing. The Police Scientific Development Branch of the Home Office had conducted a two-year review which now, again in my view and in hindsight, was most definitely flawed. Its introduction was with the intention of improving both efficiency and police-public relations. But it did exactly the opposite and eventually separated the roles of beat constable with the function of preserving close relations with the local community, and the panda car which offered a 24-hour emergency service. The criticisms which resulted, remain to this day in that when resources are stretched, the activity that always came to be reduced was preventative foot patrol.

The new Panda Car / Unit Beat Police system worked well for a few years. But it was never going to be converted back to anything which put policemen back to walking their beats. To fully enable readers to understand, it would really be advantageous to search the below link into any browser. It is a short film presented by the then Director of the Police Scientific and Development Branch. It's very much outdated now, but is an excellent view just to learn how and why it, the Panda car in particular, changed the effects of community policing.

https://www.youtube.com/watch?v=OLPjrhM4X-w

For those unable to open the link, following two years of research, the concept was arrived at, that although the community constable became a friend to the community and the community were often helpful to him, the constable on the beat contributed little to the prevention of crime and without any appreciable effect on crime detection. This, as opposed to a conspicuous patrol vehicle which would do the work of five uniformed patrols. And so it was that , UBP was introduced in order to employ a more efficient deployment of manpower through mobilisation. So now we have moved on from my 'Ringed Doughnut' concept to the below diagram spanning out from the centre – or in this case, the police station or control in the shape of a pizza slice. (Sorry) This

140

is better explained in the diagram below. By helpful coincidence, I was on the very first shift to drive Panda cars in Hereford and that happened on 1st August 1967 when I was almost 23 years of age. We were so pleased that we could give our feet and legs a rest. However, I moved to Worcester 'C' Division as a patrol sergeant in 1969 and still, the system was in its infancy but working very well. I suspect now that I was blinded by the effects it would have by in part, the fact that Worcester had been a 'City' force with plenty of police officers to deploy. Recruitment to these small forces had never been an issue. This was the prime reason why in Herefordshire and other county forces, we struggled to recruit.

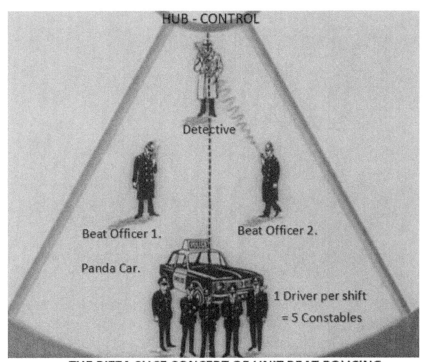

THE PIZZA SLICE CONCEPT OF UNIT BEAT POLICING

Whilst a few beat officers left their 'community beats', by and large, we had sufficient personnel to maintain community beat officers who were supplemented by 'Panda Car' patrols. But it mattered not where it was provided, the concept was as described in this above diagram. However, whilst the status quo could be managed for a longer period than in most other urban areas, the 'levelling out' of personnel at Worcester eventually caught up there which took the icing off the cake. In any event, whilst the panda car was present around the clock, the two beat officers upon which the panda car was superimposed, were only working eight-hour shifts and of course were required to take their two consecutive rest days. So, very often it was just one beat officer and a panda car on duty. Not considering absences such as rest days, training, holidays, and sickness, more often than not, the panda driver could be working alone. The detective assigned to cover both beats never applied at both Hereford and Worcester and if they were, they just merged into those detectives working from the centre.

The Ford Anglia type used at Hereford

One of the better effects of this system was that the Resident Beat Officers equipped with radios, had no reason to travel into the centre to book on duty. He would be updated by his sergeant, or an officer called a 'collator' who was responsible for receiving and disseminating information received at the centre or from other RBOs. The PSDB had calculated that for every three-foot beats (RBOs) only ten officers would be required instead of 15, a saving of five officers for every three beats. Hmmm! No matter how many it saved I doubt whether they had even considered the effect on this system when chief constables no longer had the power to direct where their officers lived. Of

142

course, one never knew what the future would bring, and I suppose that which we were experiencing at the time would, so we thought, never change.

An RBO booking on duty from his home with his radio

By that time, the police accommodation provided from the end of the war had all been built and all their RBO officers were housed in them. But as time progressed, many were occupied for the sake of occupying them and not for the purpose they were built, i.e. operational duties and when the opportunity came along for them to purchase their own, those that did caused the police houses to remain unoccupied. That is a matter which I shall deal with later at the appropriate time in Chapter 16 but so far as UBP is concerned, the concept was completely broken, and it was not long before beat officers (RBOs) were a thing of the past.

The mould of policing as previously described, suddenly changed out of all recognition. It was not as if the structure of the 'doughnut' was to change a great deal, it was the method of policing them which did. Generally, those in the centre urban areas were always on foot and those working a Resident Beat (the shaded section with RBO indicated) would either be on foot or a cycle. The problem started through that shaded 'eating part' of the doughnut which surrounded the urban hole in the centre, slowly expanding outwards as the housing stock expanded and populations increased. It was also difficult to cover for incidents on a resident beat when that officer was off duty. To expect his neighbouring resident beat officers to cover for him was a tall order because they would all be very busy and urgent calls required immediate attention. Drivers would be able to support their RBOs as a team and when they were off duty, they attend any incidents on them. That was the intention – But the idea was that the car would work with the beat officers – NOT instead of them!

The combination of reducing the areas covered by resident beat officers and increasing their number by re-aligning their boundaries was not feasible either because, due to fiscal restraints, the policing establishments of each force were not increasing to match that expansion. To repeat, the required detective constable on each area never materialised and in respect of the 'Collator', that duty should have been performed by a sergeant controller, but it was invariably a senior constable. The problem of a lack of resources was not just a local problem because all areas of the UK were similarly tasked with overcoming what was now, a national problem. The changes which then occurred were so vast as to require a completely different mould. The old mould was now to become completely smashed beyond repair. Panda cars and the concept of Unit Beat Policing were here to stay (well, for the time being) but we were required to 'make do' with the resources we had.

Communications:

All patrolling officers within quite a range of the central 'urban' police stations were issued with portable UHF radios. These would not only cover the central areas but with luck, the furthest resident beat officer from it.

This was such a leap of modernisation that any downsides would become bearable. One of them was that the radios comprised of two small units. One was to talk into, and the other was to receive messages. They were made by Pye and their profits must have shot over the top of the graph whilst the profitability of the manufacturers of Dr. Marten's Police boots took a massive tumble as shoe rubber / leather was not wearing down as fast as it had been.

For Dr Marten's sake, I just add that they changed tack and now produce what they call 'police tactical' footwear. Task Force, firearms and dog section officers can be seen wearing them, but they are not the best footwear for driving Panda Cars or any vehicle for that matter.

So far as the radios were concerned, the button seen on the side by the model's thumb below, required to be pressed as one spoke. On pressing it, an aerial would shoot up at some speed to about 6 inches from within the unit. This was pressed back into the housing after the transmission was finalised. Officers joked that it would not be long before someone's eye would be out, or the button at the top of the aerial would be lodged up noses. Of course, they had to be carried and the receiver was designed with that large clip seen in the photograph which could keep it relatively well attached to the lapels of an officer's outer garment. The transmitter would need to be carried in a bag or pocket. In our panda cars, many were damaged when on dashboards, they slid from side to side as vehicles changed direction. Whatever, the barrier of not being able to communicate with colleagues or the police station had finally been overcome. Oh, what a blessing that was.

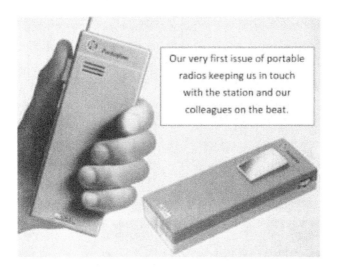

Our very first issue of portable radios keeping us in touch with the station and our colleagues on the beat.

It is also good to hear that the use of local police radio systems has once again been vastly improved. Perhaps the greatest improvement has been the fact that supervisors can now listen in to conversations and can assist with making decisions. We did not realise it then, but this mobility was the thin edge of the wedge which drove our beat constables away from their communities. It was no longer necessary to spread them wide and far to cover every inch of their individual patrols when the panda cars could get there faster anyway! So, what could possibly go wrong? So far as the drivers were concerned, they had been blessed with not requiring those big clumsy boots in which to mundanely patrol their beats on foot. They could be tucked up in their nice warm panda cars in all that rain and cold weather. On the face of it, this was marvellous. To quote the prime minister, Harold McMillan, "We had never had it so good". Sadly, he being a politician, the words soon faded away as did the notion that this new policing initiative was going to just supplement the beat officers working and chatting among their community beats. In short, panda cars should have been an additional layer on top of the RBOs on their estates. It should not have been a surprise that these cars were being deployed just about everywhere and to everything. They were darting around like the proverbial 'blue arsed flies', and oh, by the way, who was going to do the paperwork derived from the many incidents they attended? This was where the good management of these matters might well have allayed the confusion. Panda drivers did not want to get bogged down with too much paperwork and resident beat officers did not want to be landed with a pile of administration about things they had not dealt with when not on duty, or which were unconnected to their 'patch' when they returned to duty. With time increasing the workload, this developed into a complete jungle. Some of the resident beat officers would want to deal with matters which they ought to know about, particularly the miscreants on their patch. But of course, neither they nor the Panda car drivers could pick and choose. This called for some sharp supervision, but in many cases, it was not forthcoming. Murphy's law dictated that Unit Beat Policing also coincided with the period when our old sergeants with their old ways of discipline were retiring fast and us new sprogs were taking their place without the same success.

Incidents were being attended by anyone available and invariably, that was the 'Panda Car'. This became a situation which led to the term, 'Fire Brigade Policing'. That needs no explanation really but whatever is in a reader's mind, it amounted to utter confusion and our community bobbies were soon to disappear. Because of the pressure of work, short cuts were being taken to rid one job to carry on to the next one. Staff shortages never helped this situation but the saddest of all the affects was that the community's bobby was being lost. People could only see the Panda car as it whizzed by them and the housing situation to be discussed in the next chapter was to contribute to the problem despite being another benefit to the occupiers of those 'Resident Beats'.

Any new system in any environment will have its teething problems and Unit Beat Policing was no exception. For a start, the wearing of our headgear whilst driving these vehicles was never considered. We were initially told to wear our helmets but of course, they were slung in back seats of the cars until caps were issued. These too ended up on back seats and before you knew it, officers were attending incidents, jumping out of their cars without wearing any headgear at all. It was then that one realised that when being worn, the traditional police helmet played a large part in officers looking the part and gaining the respect of the public.

The village constables were still in situ for many years. I was fully aware of that because on 7th December 1970, I was posted from being a patrol sergeant in the city of Worcester to being a Rural Section sergeant at Alfrick Police Station which was a village police station in the middle of rural Worcestershire. My job as a rural section sergeant was to supervise five other village police stations and their occupants, each a constable who when on duty, would work on a 24-hour basis. There were two other similar sections, each with a sergeant in charge of a similar number of village police stations. When combined, we completely circled the rural areas surrounding Worcester from the boundaries of the resident beat officers' beats to our divisional boundary. In short, no matter in which direction you drove out of Worcester, you were bound to drive into a village in which lived a constable in a village police station which would have been supervised by one of us three sergeants. We were called the 'Worcester County Sub Division'. Unfortunately, we were only there for 17 months when thanks to some lucky crime detections when working with my beat officers, I was posted to Halesowen as a Detective Sergeant and then in

1974, I received my promotion and became an Operations Room Inspector. For the first time in uniform, I was not a community police officer. Village police stations were still in operation then, as they were for some years and some of them were now to be equipped with low powered motorcycles.

However, we moved into an era which will be better explained in the next chapter, but before leaving the subject of rural beat policing, I need to agree with those who offered me their views that it was a cushier job than being on shifts in Worcester City. Yes, I was so pleased to come off those shifts and I felt a great deal better but do not forget, each village beat officer was on duty for the whole time unless he was on a rest day. They and I could be called out at any time during those 24 hours that we were on duty and we frequently were.

I can guarantee that they were kept busy with various matters, and the huge benefit was, that they would eventually get to know just about everyone on their patch. It was because of this visibility that most crimes reported were detected. Crimes and other matters are no longer reported with such confidence because those with a need question the worth of their reports if nothing is seen to be done about them. The importance of the presence of these officers in rural areas is many but above all, they were the bridge between the police and community and the 'sounding board' of what was going on. They were, after all, VISIBLE and members of the public could call at the station to report things.

I was aware that after I had left Alfrick, another sergeant took my place but following his retirement, both houses were sold. As will be discussed in the next chapter, the selling of village police stations was performed on an incremental basis when officers were posted or simply retired, they were all eventually sold off, many, to those who then occupied them. This procedure was soon extended to the resident beat officers on estates and now I can drive around Worcester observing the many old police houses all of which are similarly designed and all displaying their Worcester City Police Crests attached like medals denoting their real contribution of the past.

Having now looked back and with my two-year secondment to the Home Office completed, I can now visualise exactly what went on. The temptation to sell off all those resident and village police houses must have been far too strong to resist for the sake of the benefits of community policing. How sad that era was when chief constables were all short of money and they were given authority, nay encouraged, to sell off the family silver which these houses then represented. Why on earth didn't they realise that we would end up in the pickle that we now have found policing in. Perhaps they had not realised it, but I am guessing that short term benefits would have blinded long term falls because all of them would be retired before that heartache was to be felt and now we are left without a real community police service.

In retrospect, I also feel it was unfortunate that we lost those old sergeants who had been bred on discipline but after all, we were now paying for being a police service and not a police force. Brain was starting to rule over brawn and it was not necessary any more to salute inspectors and above or call them 'Sir'. It was not, however, just their discipline that we missed. (If that was missed at all). It was their expertise because now, we had young sergeants (and I was the youngest) who did not have their management skills (for the want of a better word) nor their experience, but although I say it myself, I did possess some common sense and I felt that I got on OK. The blind had started leading the blind and when that happens, mayhem occurs, and it did. There was no going back.

16. Police Accommodation Part 2

The Changing Rules

It was that landmark chapter in police history triggered by Home Office Circular 300/1944, which, at the end of WW2, so wisely facilitated the building of police houses on the new housing estates then being built that makes me now return to that subject. Who could have foreseen that such an effective means of community policing would only last not even fully for two decades. A great deal of water had flowed under bridges between that time in 1950 when policemen were moving into estate houses and when we began to witness the ills of community policing around the 1970s. I consider that we had had the best of policing during those 20 years and with that in mind, I thought it necessary to continue describing the characteristics and elements comprising everyday policing then, within the last six chapters and in chronological order, before we reached the period which for me, was the beginning of the end of community policing.

It so happens that as my research has unfolded, a positive picture was emerging for police officers occupying them and subsequently for the local authorities who eventually shelved themselves of the financial burden of maintaining those police houses. From the police officers' points of view, changes in legislation permitted police officers to purchase their own houses which, in many cases took them away from their communities being policed. What was good for the goose was also good for the gander, but it was the 'community' as a whole which suffered when police officers moved out and Local Authorities sold their police houses.

This chapter in police history turned when our panda cars were operating across the country and coincidentally, the occupants of council houses were suddenly being afforded the opportunity to buy them at discounted rates provided they had resided in them for a stated number of years. Local authorities in partnership with the government had done their bit post war in being foresighted enough to realise that additional houses were required. Post war house building was a part of the progressive, establishment of the welfare state in Britain. The housing stock was considered very inadequate, and WW2 damage obviously didn't help but it was not only the quality that was the problem, the lack of numbers of adequate housing had to be addressed quickly. Obsolete housing was to be demolished and diseases such as cholera, dysentery and typhoid were all propagated by overcrowding, poor sanitation and pollution. These new estates provided that opportunity to place community police officers in police accommodation on new estates and to that end, the Government and Police Authorities were to be commended for this initiative. It was the Housing Act of 1980 which provided for council house tenants to buy the houses they occupied at a discount provided they had resided in them for a given number of years. Police houses were owned by the Local Authority so how could their police officer tenants be dealt with differently to others?

The next chapter in this 'not so sudden death' of community policing occurred on 21st December 1983 in the House of Commons when MP Eldon Griffiths made a proposal that 'whenever a 'Police Authority' owned house becomes surplus to the operational requirements of the police service in that area, it shall be the duty of that police authority to offer any police officer who is resident in that house, or in any other house provided to him by the police authority, a right to buy the house which is surplus'. They would also receive the same discount as afforded to council house tenants. It was ironic that he suggested that these houses were in bad 'ghetto' type areas which isolated them and their occupants from the rest of communities. The fact that they were in such areas, had a huge effect on community policing as was intended when plans emerged to build them. But Eldon Griffiths was the spokesman for the Police Federation, and he proffered that the trend in the rest of the population should be followed in that those officers occupying them should be able to move from their provided accommodation to home ownership.

I mentioned how 'ironic' it was because such a move would annihilate what we had come to know as 'Community Policing'. The sting in the tail was, of course a financial one in that in support of his proposal, he advised that the Police Advisory Board had identified important financial savings that could be made by reducing the housing stocks held by police authorities. Savings on maintenance and replacement could also be enjoyed. His father had been a Police Sergeant and he was the member of parliament who was representing the rank and file of the membership of the Police Federation. (Up to Chief Inspector) I may be cynical but suspect that it would have been the benefit to those police officers he represented which was the main cause that had driven him. At the same time, he would not be losing the financial savings present to the Local Authorities and Home Office. **YES, IT WAS MUCH TO DO WITH COST CUTTING AND LITTLE DID HE KNOW THEN, WHAT A DISASTER TO COMMUNITY POLICING THAT WOULD BRING – POLITICIANS MESSING WITH THE POLICE AGAIN!**

Here was an open invitation to leave these areas without being policed. They could **not** possibly be described as anything but 'OPERATIONALLY REQUIRED'. Eldon Griffiths' proposal went through many amendments but as time progressed, what then happened is now history.

Fast forward sixteen years with no attention being paid to 'Operational Necessity' when police officers were then able to purchase these houses, the proposition was described as a 'win-win' affair and so, the sale of surplus police houses had then become a regular practice of most forces. BUT, whilst this was an alleged win-win situation, it had been forgotten that all that was involved in this process, comprised three elements – they were: -

1. The Police Authority that owned these houses.
2. The Police Officers who occupied them.
3. The people of the communities who were policed by the occupants.

It was not a Win-Win-Win situation – But the question was – Who Cared? The third element of this tripartite affair was the community, and they would not feel the effects until their communities started to miss their local bobby and he was not concerned at all because now he was able to buy his own house. The wrongdoers on these estates were very happy at the expense of their law-abiding neighbours. It was stated that there were then, hundreds and perhaps thousands of police houses that were surplus to operational requirements and that whether such houses were surplus would rest with the individual Chief Officer. With their miss match of ideas, came a lengthy levelling out period until eventually, all were sold.

The death knell had just about chimed for police provided accommodation and more importantly, community policing and specifically the policing of the 'not so good' estates with bad reputations. I would wager that any officer joining the force in my time and beyond had no idea that they were given a police house or paid a rent allowance merely because the Chief Officer could direct them to live and work wherever he thought prudent. It was just regarded as a heaven-sent perk of the job, or so we thought. It must be acknowledged however, that many a new police station has been built within forces with the capital derived from the sale of police houses. It is just a pity and so ironic that many of them have now been closed. And by the same token, who can blame the resident police officers in them, for buying their houses at handsome discounts?

Whatever the situation, our police were now very much more mobile with rural areas beyond urban areas of towns and their estates, being reached far quicker than the village bobby could get his cycle clips on. All true, but no-one had taken account of the vast amount of intelligence and general information gleaned from those villages and estates who lost their constables as they policed those areas, let alone the confidence and trust in the police which was bound to wane without the relationship existing between them. I repeat what I've said before, you cannot measure prevention, you can measure crime increases and decreases but you cannot measure how many crimes were prevented by a visible police presence and this may have influenced the judgement of the 'Police Research and Scientific Development Branch' who did not understand the value of community policing when they conducted their two years of research.

Law abiding members of the community served had become the friend of the bobby on their beat and in short, that is when I contend that we lost 'Community Policing' and the confidence in the police which was once held very much to our benefit. The 'Unit Beat Policing' system with all its 'Panda Cars' would have continued to work very well if only police resources had been supplied to maintain it. The cost cutting benefits had obviously been used elsewhere and not where it mattered so far as 'law and order' was concerned.

There were transitional arrangements made to replace 'Rent Allowances' from 1st April 1990 but that was abolished for new recruits and frozen for serving officers from 1 September 1994, because police officers were no longer required to live in a particular location. The structure of starting salaries changed as a result but I was oblivious of this situation then as my retirement came along just two months later! So, without any of us feeling the pain and without any resistance made, police authorities no longer had the burden of maintaining police accommodation. This of course, meant that so long as they could do their job efficiently, officers could live virtually wherever they wished and in their own property. No doubt an understanding was made of operational requirements in the early days of this transition but unless I am mistaken, there are very few, if any at all, village police stations left, and we are without any residential beat officers patrolling our estates.

I mentioned earlier that reviews of the organisation and structure of our police service was something we were required to endure throughout our service, very often when changes of the management structure occurred. 1991 was no exception because in August of that year, David Blakey took the Chief Constable's chair from Tony Mullett who was appointed as the first director of the 'National Criminal Intelligence Service' (NCIS). The review had probably commenced in Mr Mullett's stewardship but whatever, the demise of our 'Estate Police' and subsequently our village police stations naturally resulted in all the management segments (Divisions and Sub Divisions) of our police areas having to rely on 'the centre' urban police to operate in mobiles. Although not a prime reason, it would obviously be more prudent to reduce the areas of those segments to reduce the time taken to reach their boundaries. This was just one of other benefits and so, the structure was changed from six Divisions to nine Sub Divisions each being a 'Basic Command Unit' operating with devolved budgets and under the command of a Superintendent. The Sub Divisions were in turn, spread into three large areas each under the command of Area Chief Superintendents. The demise of this estate and rural policing was similarly dealt with in other forces.

Chief Officers were virtually swept along with the tide. It was said that due to the increase in the workload, a balance was required between urban and rural policing. My view was that this was 'shorthand writing' for 'response policing from the centre'. (Fire Brigade Policing) It does not take much calculating that the immeasurable benefits of community policing with its preventive patrol was sacrificed for putting all our police eggs into one basket at the larger 24-hour police stations. English policing was to become a response thing and it wasn't long before we heard cries of, "Put our police back on the beat"!

It was the review that, in 1993, also saw responsibility for road traffic policing to be a Sub Divisional responsibility by using Sub Divisional Response Vehicles (SDRVs) which were renamed 'Sub Divisional Traffic Cars' coming under direct control of Sub Divisional Commanders but receiving a 'Traffic Steer' from HQ. Traffic policing with larger, more high-speed vehicles had remained under the umbrella of the three Traffic Areas. Panda cars were being replaced by slightly more powerful vehicles called 'Response Vehicles' because now they needed to get everywhere from their central hub at faster speeds on longer journeys. Mass shooting tragedies around the country saw the additional requirement for some specialised response vehicles to be equipped with firearms and some drivers were required to be 'Class A' drivers in addition to being firearms trained.

So, without visualising the long-term effects, it appeared then, that everyone was happy with this reactive policing. It was a victory so far as the domestic arrangements for officers were concerned because it allowed our officers to be released from the manacles which tied them to live where they were told to live. They were now also allowed to purchase their own homes. But from a policing point of view, we were not going to shout about it because, although not immediately identified then, it was one of the most disastrous moves that affected the local policing of our communities. For those that thought they won, it was good but not for all concerned. The ripples would not be reaching the banks of the pond until sometime later. But what can be done about those negative effects, now that the ripples have reached the water's edge?

Whatever I say here, will most probably not be given any credibility by those who may possess the wherewithal to instigate such a reversal. In fact, reversing to that era would, in my view, not be possible. However, it cannot be beyond the wit of man (or woman) to provide some kind of policing to these estates and I offer the following for consideration: -

- There are now 'Community Housing Associations' in being to bring those less fortunate closer to house ownership. So surely, some kind of assistance could be provided by Police Authorities (Now of course, Police Commissioners holding purse strings) so that added contracts could be made with officers who find it beyond their financial reach to find deposits to purchase their own. I have not obviously thought out the minutia of a scheme, but it would be based on the possibilities of the much sought-after deposit to purchase property, being loaned to the officer at a discounted repayment aligned to their salary.
- As hinted above, the PCSO schemes now in existence, could be extended to in effect, convert them to becoming community constables. Let them, or the best of them, take the oath, provide the uniforms, and train and pay them as police officers. Those I have met in research and discussed policing with, seem very capable and that would also bring us policing with that microcosm of society that is drifting away from us. I can foresee the time when regionalisation will take care of serious crime including drugs offences and cybercrime and other major crimes. In effect, a two-tier system of policing could take care of the 'lower' tier of community crime whilst an extension of the 'National Crime Agency' could be left to deal with the serious.
- I consider that insufficient thought has been given to the role of the Special Constabulary. Why don't we see them or police volunteers on patrol in our villages and estates. There are huge holes to be filled.
- Although flying in the face of proposed graduate entry schemes, there are bound to be suitable persons on large estates who would be willing to be recruited into the police to be based on where they currently reside as did our

now extinct RBOs. Let's find these people, train, and equip them and have them police their own estates. In effect, pay them to stay where they are, in exchange for their paid police cover.

In researching this problem, I was particularly taken with an American idea operated by the US Department of Housing and Urban Development (HUD) which came to fruition because of the same problem. It is called, 'Good Neighbour Next Door'. Law enforcement officers, teachers, firefighters, and emergency medical technicians can contribute to community revitalisation while becoming homeowners through this scheme which offers a substantial incentive in the form of a discount of 50% from the list price of the home. In return, an eligible buyer must commit to live in the property for 36 months as his/her principal residence. Eligible family homes located in revitalisation areas are listed exclusively for sale through the scheme. HUD requires that applicants sign a 2nd mortgage and note for the discount amount. No interest or payments are required on this "silent second" mortgage provided that the three-year occupancy requirement is fulfilled.

Full details can be found at the link - https://www.hud.gov/abou

The overall objective is, to return to preventive policing in that we must get our patrolling officers back to working into these problematic estates from where they could police adjoining villages in addition to their own community beats. I see no point at all for writing the gobbledegook currently written about how much community policing is valued if the solution remains that it can be achieved by paying spasmodic visits to meetings at a village hall which are now more frequently not attended by the police and if they were, would only be attended by law abiding citizens. We must get among those we need to effect, not the already converted!

One retired officer who purchased his old village police station wrote to me that his door was continuously knocked for five years after it had been purchased by him. Callers gazed at him incredulously when they were told that they had to report such issues to the city station many miles away.

If this chapter has done anything at all, I trust that it identifies the fact that at least the conditions officers now work under, have improved to such an extent that by and large, they are able to buy their own house if they can. That is an achievement but however, with prices now increased out of reach for most in society these days, many might well have preferred to turn the clock back to live rent free. Pie in the sky I know, but it would also re-set the concept of 'community policing'. I wish!

I was so shocked to suddenly realise that all our current police officers and their chief constables will be in a position unable to truly understand what has been missed because all of them now, will not have been aware of the system before they joined. Regrettably the 'response' type policing is and will always be the normal method of policing they only understand, and which carries no preventive measures at all. That and the camaraderie and moral of officers is what is now sadly missing and for me, the two most important achievable objectives. When police clubs closed and briefing parades were discontinued, we had no idea how camaraderie and hence, morale would have suffered. We need to re-set our policing back into a 'Vocation' and not just 'A Job' as it has been turned into today.

17. Brighter Stars of the Future?

Having not exactly declared my support for the lack of action detected in those gobbledegook objectives, policies or statements referred to in many of the above chapters, I was quite heartened when I discovered the ideas emanating from the 'Police Foundation'. I had heard of this agency but had never had the need, or more likely had bothered, to explore it. And, though I suspect that it has no 'teeth', I am more than pleased that I have.

The **Police Foundation** describes itself as the UK's policing 'think tank' and being the only independent body in the UK that research, understands and works to improve policing for the benefit of the public. In other words, it is a good conduit into those who have the teeth. Wow, this sounded very much like a description of a body that, unlike those pledges contained in the masses of gobbledegook I had hitherto ploughed through, might just be positive enough to produce ideas which could well amount to helping those 'Left Behind Communities' to recapture the community policing that had dwindled over years past. Wikipedia tells me that this organisation had hosted several of policing and criminal justice inquiries and reviews which included a '2019 Strategic Review of Policing in England and Wales'. This had been the first fundamental review of policing for many years, and it was conducted by its chair, Sir Michael Barber.

Here I found a rare document that was gobbledegook free and contained many practical recommendations with which I thought could succeed to making successful differences. However, I was never going to hold my breath because, unless the implementation clock needed repair, I had heard nothing of any progress in relation to the implementation of any of the recommendations.

With a sense of excitement, I immediately contacted Richard James FRSA who, whilst I plead guilty to some nepotism here, is not only a retired senior police officer with a keen interest in turning the key to crime prevention and other social and policing issues, is also my son-in-law. I swear that I did not influence this union with my daughter, and I did not even know that he was a police officer until she informed me and came to pick her up in an old Porsche car!!!

Although from different generations, we naturally discuss such matters, but I hasten to add that even with a common interest, we have never worked together or collaborated in any way. We both share a concern at the dwindling visibility and the ineffectiveness of the police and thus possess a common interest in improving the situation. Together with Tim Curtis FRSA, a senior lecturer in social innovation at Northampton University, they developed a company, 'Intensive Engagement' designed to engage with communities and reduce crime. Richard is the managing director and after ten years of success with police and local authorities, they have realised that the concept they promulgate, can be spread across communities to capture the talents of volunteers and other public and private agencies and organisations to tackle this growing problem, all of which, are aimed at improving lives in our more crime ridden society.

I emphasise here that we have never worked together on such enterprises and of course, he being one generation behind me, our views and past police experiences will inevitably differ to produce different ideology though both seeking to score the same goals. My interest is confined to writing about what I consider is a social history chapter and I am not therefore concerned in any business.

I regard myself as being fortunate in experiencing such a wide parameter of policing change encompassing the period from 1960 until almost this second decade of the 21st century. Anyway, it was Richard who confirmed that the Police Foundation might be very useful in my quest and he suggested that some of my thirst would be quenched by a particular member of the foundation, a certain Andy Higgins.

And so, having now researched more closely, the activities of the Police Foundation and its latest review, I cannot think of anything better at this juncture, to make comment on at least the recommendations of the review and later, the pertinent topics of Andy Higgins.

Strategic Review of Policing 2019. (Sir Michael Barber)

As the heading suggests, this is a comparatively recent review and was the first of its kind for many years. It was guided by an advisory board of former senior police officers, politicians, and leading academics. The overall aim of the review was to set a long-term strategic vision for English and Welsh policing. Whilst it was inevitable that the board would contain politicians and academics, it was almost unusual in my estimation, that it contained some practitioners of former senior police officers. I just hope that they were not too former, like me! Sir Michael made 56 recommendations for a modern police service capable of meeting the challenges of the 21st century and whilst I shall not go into all of them, I will include those here which after all, will be among the very rare examples of what I call achievable features and not just the clearing of the rubble along the path which leads us to them.

In launching the Review's final report at an event in London, **Sir Michael Barber** said: -

> *"There is a crisis of confidence in policing in this country which is corroding public trust. The reasons are deep rooted and complex – some cultural and others systemic. However, taken together, unless there is urgent change, they will end up destroying the principle of policing by consent that has been at the heart of British policing for decades.*

> *"Policing in this country is at a crossroads and it cannot stand still whilst the world changes so quickly around it. Now is the moment to move forward quickly on the path of reform. The warning signs if we do nothing are flashing red and we ignore them at our peril.*

> *"This report represents the most comprehensive review of policing for a generation and sets out an agenda for fundamental change. It is the product of over two years of work and engagement with the police and a range of different*

stakeholders. Everyone recognises the need to shift the odds, which too often are stacked in favour of the criminal. We need a modern police service fit for the future which is at the cutting edge of technology and training. And we need it urgently. I believe the will is there and that the talented police officers who work tirelessly for the public would be the strongest champions of change."

So, with his words fitting exactly with my sentiments, without blandly copying the recommendations as made, I simply reproduce the main thrust of them as summarised in their publication to the media. The added comment made since their publication, is also most useful: -

- o   Creation of a new Crime Prevention Agency.
- o   Expansion of the role of the National Crime Agency so it in effect becomes a new FBI for the UK.
- o   Introduction of a new licence to practice for all police officers that is renewed every five years and subject to strict conditions.
- o   Merger of back-office functions across the 43 forces that would save hundreds of millions of pounds.
- o   Investment in front line policing, training, and technology to modernise the service from top to bottom.

The review found that the police service has not kept pace with the changing patterns of crime while also having to deal with huge rises in non-crime related demand:

- o   In 2021, 53% of all crime affecting people in England and Wales was fraud and cybercrime. Despite this, just 0.1% result in a charge or summons.

- o   There has been a 240% increase in the numbers of rapes reported to the police and yet the percentage of rape cases resulting in a charge fell from 8.5% in 2015 to just 1.5% in 2021.

- o Detection rates generally have almost halved in the last seven years, falling from 17% all reported crimes resulting in a charge or summons in 2014 to just 9% today.

- o There was a 28% increase in mental health related incidents between 2014 and 2018 across 26 forces.

- o Around three million 'investigation hours' are dedicated to missing persons reports very year, the equivalent of 1,562 full time police officers per year or the number of police officers needed for North Yorkshire.

As a result, the report argues that the public is losing confidence:

- o The proportion of crime victims who were 'very satisfied' with the police response declined from 42% in 2014 to 32% in 2020, while the proportion 'not satisfied' rose from 26% to 34%.

- o Between 2016 and 2020 the proportion of people saying they thought the police did a good or excellent job fell from 63% to 55%.

To tackle this crisis of confidence and ensure the police service can meet the challenges of the future, the report calls for radical reform to three broad areas of police-public relations, skills and training, and organisation.

Police-public relations

There needs to be an improvement in the relationship between the police and the public. The report includes a series of recommendations including:

- o An increase in visible **neighbourhood policing** in every police force.

- o Improved **training and support for sergeants and inspectors** so they are equipped to provide stronger supervision, tackle poor conduct, and call out bad behaviour.

- ○ National targets to improve the **diversity of the police workforce**. At the current pace of change it will take another 58 years (until 2079) for the police service to achieve a workforce that is representative of England and Wales in terms of ethnicity.

Skills and Training

Police training needs a complete overhaul so that the police are equipped to take on new forms of crime. 40% of police officers say they had not received necessary training to do their job well. The report includes a series of recommendations to improve this including:

- ○ Action to tackle a shortage of 6,851 detectives across the country, including expanded **direct entry schemes** to attract mid-career applicants from other sectors and **a new pay supplement** to attract more officers into investigatory roles. *(Inserted - OH, WHAT DOES THIS TELL US? I cannot agree to 'Direct Entry' to CID)*

- ○ Every officer should be entitled to a minimum set of hours per year reserved for **learning and development**.

- ○ The Home Office should introduce a **Licence to Practice** for police officers, administered by the College of Policing. This should be renewed every five years, subject to an officer demonstrating professional development through achieving relevant qualifications, passing an interview, or presenting a portfolio of activities and achievements. Any police officer who fails this assessment could receive further support including mentoring. After successive failures they would have their licence removed and would no longer be able to practice as a police officer. **(Inserted: The annual appraisal was hugely time consuming. Has that gone? If not or even if so, this licence will involve and abstract a great deal of time to implement and would require separate resourcing.**

Organisation

The way the police service is organised has not changed significantly since the 1960s. Local police forces should focus on local crime, emergency incidents and visible community policing. They are however poorly equipped to tackle surging levels of fraud and cybercrime. It is neither effective nor efficient for every police force to run its own HR, finance and other support functions.

The report makes several recommendations to reform the way the police service is organised including:

- To tackle surging levels of fraud and cybercrime, the government should introduce a dedicated **Crime Prevention Agency** that would be responsible for ensuring crime is designed out at source. This new Agency would have powers to enforce a new statutory duty on large companies to prevent crime.

- To tackle increasing levels of cross border crime there should be a **major expansion of the National Crime Agency (NCA),** to make it more like a British FBI. Regional Organised Crime Units (ROCUs), which currently sit with local police forces, should be transferred over to the National Crime Agency. This would put these units on a firmer financial footing and would make sure they were housed within a national network that prioritises tackling serious and organised crime.

- The **College of Policing should be reformed and expanded** to become a powerful agency for police improvement. It should have powers to set mandatory professional standards for all police officers, to require police forces to address skills gaps and to require police forces to develop common IT standards so data can be properly shared between forces.

- Specialist and back-office functions, currently largely operating in each of the 43 forces, should be merged into **Regional Police Support Units**, which would ensure they were delivered more effectively and would save hundreds of millions of pounds in reduced duplication.

As the reader may well perceive, the main thrust of my concern throughout this book centres around the abandonment of those now 'lost communities' when it comes to 'on the ground' community policing. These recommendations were akin to taking a freshly roasted chicken out of the oven. When it cooled, you could pick the nice juicy bits off and leave behind the carcass and bits which were not going to be so tasty. I was therefore particularly pleased to see the inclusion of the '*Investment in front line policing, training and technology to modernise the service from top to bottom*' recommendation included. Additionally, the recommendation of "Local police forces should focus on local crime, emergency incidents and visible community policing" will always get my support. Of course, it would be difficult not to have included such systemic recommendations, however, to what extent will notice be taken of them is left to the imagination. Even at the time of writing this, (late 2022-23) though we are now three years behind the time of the publication of these recommendations, I cannot ascertain what, if any, progress has been achieved in their implementation. I have a feeling that the police's response will be – "Well, were just too busy doing what we can to get bogged down with implementing changes in organisation."

I do not pretend to know the answer to this but undoubtedly, this should be prioritised with maybe an outside body being funded to task building the skeletons on which the flesh could be added. Whatever, my joy was harnessed if only because of this brave attempt to put forward those seen as practical 'doable' solutions. I have been frustrated in reading the statements and policies already referred to in chapters past, but that when they are dissected, provide no hints at all as to what must be done to achieve those objectives and goals. As I keep saying, we need action, not just words. Sir Michael's recommendations are a good start, but something now needs to be done so far as prioritising and the implementation of the achievable recommendations.

So having contacted my son-in-law, Richard James and having understood what it was that I desired, he directed me to an employee at the Police Foundation, Andy Higgins who I suspect had made a considerable contribution towards the making of the Strategic Review's recommendations. Fortunately, son-in-law Richard and his company had identified the likelihood of time and funds not being made available to react to these recommendations at least, in full and they had been largely working on methods and themes which would sadly, not entirely count on them being implemented. They had designed a process to harness that which is already present within neighbourhoods but is yet untapped and which might be combined to bring them together collectively to use the leadership skills of people who, for example, lead voluntary organisations such as scouts and sports clubs as well as local authorities at maybe Parish or County levels. They could at least use their leadership skills to raise the confidence levels of communities from those levels to where they have now dropped.

I learned that great effort had been put into establishing an eight-point plan briefly described as shown here: -

1. Clarify the justification for commencing Intensive Engagement – scan what is known about the neighbourhood.
2. What community assets already exist in the location? What networks and associations are there? What are the vulnerabilities in the area?
3. Who shares the problem? Stakeholders and networks identify who are directly involved in this issue. How are all people / agencies involved, associated?
4. Develop deep community insights using Rich Pictures – Engage with community members to establish how all stakeholders see the problem? Where do the issues arise? What parts of the neighbourhood are successful? Map the results.
5. Form a working group of stakeholders who are engaged and able to make changes.
6. Develop Solution Rich Pictures – Engage the working group to identify what the solutions look like from the stakeholder's perspective? How can they be achieved? What would the neighbourhood look like if all the issues were solved?
7. Agree Interventions and Evaluation (Who is doing what, when, how, by when, what does success look like?)

8. Establish escalation processes with stakeholders, authorities and agencies. What will make the interventions fail? What are you going to do about it to prevent that happening?

It would be ideal if the police could again play a major part in these strategies but sadly, that is more than likely what has not happened in most of our troubled communities since pro-active community policing ceased but who knows, such innovations might get the horse to drink some water?

Returning to the work of Andy Higgins, Research Director at the Foundation, I discovered that his work closely resembled the policing dilemmas, its problems its successes and its failures, much along the same direction as my brain had been directing me and certainly, along the same directions as that of Richard James' Intensive Engagement. He too had also identified that Covid 19 had brought that flickering light of community spirit I have already described in my 'Community Policing' chapter above.

In a 2021 paper, titled 'POLICE IN PLACE' – Why the police need to reconnect locally, he describes the same threats, real or perceived that we all suffer from and the need in a more globalist world, for us to live in a tighter, more secure environment so that we can operate in it with more confidence. Sophisticated fraudsters, many operating 'on line', are probably a good example of this trend. In a nutshell, what Andy appears to me to be referring to, is akin to our comfort and reactions being similarly reflective of those to do with our natural sensations about, for example, our local environmental changes, such as adding housing stock to an overburdened infrastructure and maybe to us preferring locally grown produce to that which has been shipped maybe, halfway around the world.

I think his philosophy runs parallel to that which 'Intensive Engagement' discourses in that by uniting the hidden leadership talents already existing, this comfort would be similarly generated to produce a resilience which just might reignite that kind of community spirit felt during Covid 19. Those are simple examples but the overall message he proffers concerns us not curling up in a defensive ball and hoping that our increased security threats will go away. The message, to which I concur, is perhaps we should do something about it; though the aim of this book is to highlight the dismay felt by all sections of the communities in the alarming and increasing inefficiencies of the police, in the hope that something will be done about it.

After all, they are the agencies which are paid to police effectively and for which we pay most of our taxes, including our local council tax. They have all the personnel, training, tools and organisation and structure already in place. What a good start that is. I would just want them to get on with it.

As if to emphasise the importance of our police being local, Andy reminds us that it was Sir Robert Peel who organised the system of 'Local Beats' and the provision of police accommodation in the provinces which had the effect of extending the long arm of the law into them – So what has changed to make us ignore that edict? I argue that abandoning those practices was the beginning of the end of local policing and that in no time at all, we are now paying for it dearly.

He says –

> *"Along with consumer goods, recreational drugs, the end of National Service, emancipated women leaving empty homes to go to work, and rock and roll and revolution, the1960s gave the police sirens and radios, 999 call after 999 call, and new 'modern' ways of organising themselves.*
>
> *Bobbies came off the beat and climbed into panda cars. They ranged further, became less familiar, stopped policing places and started policing incidents.*
>
> *Crime continued to rise, the post-war settlement continued to unwind, and this more impersonal, less grounded police service found itself increasingly at odds with a more liberated, less deferential British public: race riots in the cities, striking miners in the provinces, corruption in the papers. There had to be a better way."*

Well, how close can that be to what I have been far less skilled at saying in those pages past. When describing the onset of community policing, he flies the flags of Sir John Alderson, the Chief Constable of Devon and Cornwall during the 1970s and early 80s, and the recommendations of Lord Scarman after the Brixton riots, but says it was not until the current millennium that concerted national efforts were made to re-root British policing.

In particular, he states that it was between 2005 and 2008 when New Labour's flagship policing reforms saw a patchwork blanket of Neighbourhood Policing teams rolled out over England and Wales. He mentions the newly created Community Support Officers playing their part in this enterprise.

I hate to disagree with him there, because although his reasoning in the solutions he writes about are so closely aligned with mine, I can assure him that between 2005 and 2008, the period he describes above, community policing had been dead for many years. It was very efficiently being practiced to huge benefits at least as far back as 1965 when every large housing estate in Hereford was being policed by a dedicated police officer residing in police owned accommodation on those estates. That was to my personal knowledge, and I believe it had been that way for many years previous to that.

Maybe that is not significant, and I am drifting off the point because Andy continues to record what effect that additional layer of police presence called 'Crime Support Officers' had. I and other interested colleagues, especially the Police Federation, were bitterly against such appointments because it was so obviously a policy for introducing them as second-class police officers who would be costing far less than those they were to replace. Whilst the pilot schemes worked well, it was not too long before, in my opinion, they too became somewhat invisible and are now, doing a good job in pushing out warnings in newsletters containing good advice about safeguarding from the tricks and scams being operated against us. However, as hinted below, much of these sorts of operations are conducted in the police stations which previously were open to the public and housed 24/7 shifts of police officers. At least that is the situation which exists in the town closest to where I reside.

What with the Traffic Wardens virtually disappeared and when the Local Authorities introduced their own car parking wardens, all that was left were those as I say, fast disappearing from sight, PCSOs.

Andy justifiably in my estimation writes: -

> *In 2018, when the Police Foundation pieced together the lost narrative of the model's post-roll-out decade, most uniformed cops (regardless of job title) were spending every rostered hour blue-lighting between emergency calls (many also carrying large caseloads of routine 'beat-crime' investigations), buffeted by an onslaught of 'demand', dealing with the urgent at the expense of the essential. Some forces even had the rhetorical temerity to rebrand their response cops as neighbourhood patrol officers (or some linguistic variant) – because everything happens someplace – Right?*

The PACE Act 1984 was not the only statute which concerned personal 'restrictive' measures to be introduced in that 1980s decade. The government became concerned that existing data protection provisions made under a Council of Europe Convention, was more to do with business than with any desire to protect personal privacy.

The Data Protection Act 1984 reached the statute book in July 1984. It established new rights for individuals, the most important of which was the right to know if an organisation was processing personal data about them and the right to have a copy of the information (the right of subject access). Individuals also had a right to complain to the Registrar who was appointed to oversee such issues. However, the provisions of this 1984 Act were limited to data stored on a computer and the enforcement regime was cumbersome. Quibbles between EU member states to make legislation on this issue uniform, finally came to rest with the introduction by the new Labour Government of the Data Protection Act 1998.

One might be asking, "What has the data protection laws got to do with policing"? It was very much highlighted during this 1998 Act's passage to the statute book that it shared common ground with the 'Human Rights Bill' and aimed to improve the rights of citizens to rely on a wide range of civil and political rights contained in the European Convention on Human Rights. It has now been amended by the 2018 Data Protection Act.

Prying into the antecedents and current private lives of many people, especially those suspected of crime, was more than a regular occurrence to all police officers. It was so easy to ring a local taxation office to ascertain the ownership of a registered vehicle. It was so easy to contact employers who were largely quite willing to pass information regarding their employees, it was so easy to tap up bank managers to divulge the comings and goings of funds in the accounts of suspects. This list could go on and on. It is of course, very easy to continue to obtain this type of information but it must be done in a more professionally structured way with the seeking of orders in many cases. Contravention is a criminal offence and many a police officer has been convicted of it and dismissed from their police force in serious breaches. It was not long before I and all other police officers had to attend remote learning lessons and qualify to receive a certificate that we had passed the 'Data Protection' course. We had all been warned and no longer were those 'picking up the phone' favours allowed.

Privacy must of course, be respected but surely the police were not asking for a 'police state' to be incorporated, they were just doing the job which detectives no longer do and maybe that is another nail in the coffin which now causes many not to be so interested in the CID as they had been. My view is that replacing them with recruits directed straight into the CID will be an absolute disaster. Yet another calamity suffered to the investigative skills which really did little or no harm in the first place.

Other statutes of the 1980s and onwards which created more dents to that method of policing and the mould of the officers policing then, are listed below and upon which I have made comment elsewhere.

- The Housing Act 1980
- The Police and Criminal Evidence Act 1984

- The Prosecutions of Offenders Act 1985- which introduced the Crown Prosecution Service
- The Human Rights Act 1988
- The Equality Act 2010 and the
- The Police Reform and Social Responsibility Act 2011 which introduced Police and Crime Commissioners.

That 1980s decade was surely a busy one for the reformers. I fully recognise that each one has been introduced with good intentions but sadly, in my opinion, so far as our policing and feeling of secureness is concerned, they, or combinations of them, have sadly caused the degree of our police efficiency and effectiveness to have sadly dropped.

I could continue with what Andy Higgins describes has happened, but it has mostly been said in previous chapters. He additionally states, "Local safety-making now meant managing high-risk offenders, protecting vulnerable victims, sorting out multi-agency service provision for 'frequent flyers' and working with troubled families. Not problems, nor places, but 'cases' were becoming the new units of police work in neighbourhoods.

He continues, "Where structures, resources, 'culture' and too many leaders with too little vision put up barriers, there are countless local heroes working around them and in between, who get it and get on with it". He continues, "They are the neighbourhood bobby with a story for every street corner, the PCSO with a name for every face and thousands of leg-miles on the clock, they are the graduate recruit who has not yet seen it all and is all the better for it, they are the analyst who can see beneath the hotspot map, the community safety officer who understands that communities make safety, the volunteer and the youth worker, the campaigner and coordinator, the historian and steward and poet of place.

Theirs are the stories that need to be shared, connected, combined, and amplified; to be heard beyond their places, so that they can inspire, engage, and empower others and provide the raw materials to craft the stories from which change is made."

My only problem remains in that I and hopefully, many thinking members of our communities understand that these resources exist and could be utilised. Richard James's 'Intense Engagement's eight-point plan could and has worked, yet whether it is resulted in that curling up into a fearful ball or not, my recent experience is that individual members are not so keen to volunteer these days as they were in the past. Those who have formed such organisations as service clubs are now dwindling to such an event that Round Tables, Rotary clubs, Lions clubs, Probus clubs and the many other similar voluntary organisations are now reducing in numbers or have folded completely as has my own Rotary Club. As was mentioned to me by that solicitor friend of mine, 'evolution, by its very definition, means 'change'.

Conversely, the Covid 19 scenario mentioned above and the rise in community volunteer run shops and food banks leaves maybe a glimmering hope for the future, but somehow, I feel that to be a distant dream as opposed to maybe that required to transform the police into what it had been in the past in terms of better leadership, camaraderie, and morale. What has fuelled those changes? Maybe the next chapter is another starter for ten?

18. The Judicial System And

The Crown Prosecution Service

So far as I can remember, the jurisdiction, purpose, and procedures of our Magistrates' courts in the modern era have been governed by legislation dating back to 1952 and many Criminal Justice Acts of the 1960s and more recently, the 'Magistrates' Courts' Act 1980. These often named 'Lower Courts' were governed by staff of the Magistrates Courts Association and for much of my police service, they were informally known as 'Police Courts' because, together with the court's staff, the police virtually operated them as they had done, since time immemorial. It had been the police who arrested suspects, the police who decided on charging or summoning them to court, and who made decisions as to whether suspects were bailed or not. Was it no wonder then, that they had been called 'Police Courts'? This control by the police had finally raised eyebrows and it had been decided that maybe a sprinkling of some form of professional independence was necessary.

Apart from cases involving vulnerable people and juveniles where maybe joint decisions were made with social services departments, the police prosecutions departments would hire local solicitors to prosecute the 'not guilty' plea cases. All other cases would normally be prosecuted by police officers, usually in my force, inspectors. In the absence of the inspector, I regularly did this at both the Droitwich and Worcester County Magistrates' courts in the rank of sergeant. Later, as an inspector at Droitwich, this was a regular duty, which I got to enjoy after being frightened to death when I first started prosecuting.

No doubt due to fiscal constraints, many courts were merged into each other causing buildings and staff losses. The nature of what had been 'Local Courts' dealing with local people, had been lost and all those people normally found in courts such as the justices, their clerks, police officers, witnesses, defendants, probation officers, newspaper reporters etc. were suddenly required to travel sometimes many additional miles.

The PACE Act had only just brought tighter controls on how suspects were treated by the police and now in 1986, this additional layer of controlling all aspects relating to the charging of suspects and the ensuing processes involved up to final court appearances had been taken out of the police's control and placed into the hands of what was to be a giant additional organisation called the 'Crown Prosecution Service' (CPS). The complete independence of the CPS was emphasised to such an extent that their offices and those of the police, were not permitted to be under the same roofs. The positive aspects of this meant that many police officers and support staff were relieved of these duties but on the other hand, it meant that suddenly, many obstacles were introduced which required jumping before suspect were charged and arraigned before a court.

The changes made affected every sinew of the processes involved in the detention, charging and final appearance of every person brought into custody. So far as the 'right of silence' is concerned, suspects have always had the right to remain silent when being questioned. However, there are special circumstances when a judge can advise a jury that they can attribute their own reasons why suspects would not want to make replies to police questioning. Bearing in mind that the CPS would only permit suspects being charged with offences if there was a reasonable chance that a prosecution would be successful, it can be imagined that a greater chance now existed, that defendants would never be charged and therefore, would never appear at a trial. So those special circumstances would, in any event, never be relied upon. In short, suspects now had a greater chance of not being charged with the offences for which they had been arrested.

If there was any doubt at all, they would not have authorised proceedings. This situation has become farcical to such an extent that although I have watched numerous 'cold case' programs together with other 'real life' police documentaries, I cannot recall many, if at all, where suspects have actually agreed to answer questions.

With the decision to grant bail now being taken out of police hands, that process will in itself, have considerably increased the suspects chances of the CPS not authorising the police to charge them. So, I'm afraid that we shall be hearing those two words even more often – 'NO COMMENT'.

On reflection now, the mid to late 1980s period had represented a mammoth change which when all considered together, saw the end of those days when suspects could be thrown into a cell on a Friday afternoon with a promise that they would be seen after the weekend during which time, they could decide on whether to "tell the truth or get remanded in custody". Whilst this (little used) practice appears barbaric now, it must be realised that most crimes were committed by a minority of families and in any event, on many occasions the police were told who the authors of crimes were. The system worked due to the relationships held between these criminal types and the local police who knew each other very well.

In the policing world, surely this was the era which represented the first ripples of the giant waves of 'Human Rights' which were to swell and later 'drown' this police control and which, of course, eventually saw the Human Rights Act 1998 appear in our statute books. I had been retired for four years then and was often working abroad being so busy that I had no idea of how police practice and procedures had been so vastly changed through these legislative changes.

Our society was changing and indeed, it had changed. Of course, most people would say "for the better" but so far as it affected the level of criminality and the effectiveness of the police to catch culprits is concerned, I can see plainly now, that the badges awarded for 'thief catching' had been withdrawn. The 'buzz' of thief catching no longer existed and when discovering this, I was absolutely flabbergasted to learn that uniformed police officers could no longer be persuaded to join the CID. I could not believe that to be true because in my day, there had been a long waiting list of them wanting to be given an opportunity to be a detective and it was more likely than not, that they had already demonstrated an aptitude for that kind of work. But now they are saying, "What's the point"?

I can now understand why it has been deemed necessary to advertise for recruits to be admitted as direct entrants into that department. Indeed, such policy was commended in Sir Michael Barber's recommendations but that was one of only few recommendations which I most definitely did not support. I guess his recommendation only resulted due to there being a dearth of volunteers for CID duty.

There had been a minority of detectives, mainly in London involved in wrongdoings during the investigation of crimes. Some of those acts were very serious ones even involving corruptions by one of the Met. Police's Commanders (Drury). What stuck in the craw of the rest of our throats was that such actions were not only wrongly carried out to clear up crimes by 'fitting up' criminals, they became so brazen that greed took over and money was changing hands to turn blind eyes thus allowing criminals to escape justice.

We can thank those wrongdoers (criminals) allegedly of the police service for turning the wheels in motion for metaphorically clasping handcuffs on all police officers firmly behind their backs whilst they investigated the 99.99% of all other cases legitimately.

The below is an excerpt from The Mail on Line 24th May 2019

Neil Root identifies the burly, obese Kenneth Drury, commander of the Flying Squad, the elite group of detectives charged with tackling serious crime, as chief among the conspirators: the rottenest apple in the barrel.

In hauling himself up the greasy pole, Drury (pictured below at Bow Street Magistrates in 1976) had no compunction in framing three men for a high-profile murder it later turned out they had not committed. He was a star of the police force, with a dozen major commendations to his name, a terrier who secured convictions, whatever the cost. But he had a dark side.

He was prone to doing favours for his friends and mixed in very dodgy company, too. Shortly after he took over at the Flying Squad in 1971, he ran into Humphreys, by then firmly established as Soho's 'Porn King', at a party. Humphreys quickly sealed their association with a 'drink' of £50 (more than £1,000 today).

Drury's police salary was £4,600 (approximately £115,000 today), but this was more than doubled by the £100 a week he now got from Humphreys in return for keeping the Flying Squad out of his business....

I can remember these cases very well because Drury was not the only 'bent' very senior officer to be embroiled in this messy business and television documentaries have since been published everything about them.

The whole process of the skills used in catching criminals had been put to the sword due to that minuscule minority of those so called 'bent' coppers. We have paid dearly for the actions of those who thought that by bending the rules 'just a little' was the honourable 'Noble Cause' process to detect crime and put those who committed it, behind bars. I am sure that in 99% of such small numbers, there was so called 'honour' intended but as always, there would have been others who were not so honourable. A 2010 study I came across on the Internet by a Dr Bruce Bayley who, speaking of 'Ethics in Law Enforcement' states –

Remember, we are talking about good officers trying to do the right thing (noble cause), but due to bureaucratic red tape, a lack of evidence, or any other roadblock to "getting the job done," they feel forced to bend or even break the rules to catch the bad guy (corruption). The bottom line: noble cause corruption — and thus, teleological ideologies in general — dramatically increase the likelihood of a serious situation that could easily turn horribly messy, ending your career in law enforcement and, potentially, scarring or ending the lives of you and/or others. So, what do you do when faced with the temptation of 'noble cause' corruption? The answer is simple: Remember your training!

He obviously concludes that the 'Ends do not Justify the Means'.

The tide had turned and now, resulting from the medicine prescribed to all of us in the form of PACE, its restrictions were so rigid that they took away not just the opportunities to do wrong, but by overprescribing the medication, the pendulum of justice had inevitably immediately swung far too far towards that of the accused and of course, that could only encourage the commission of more crime. What a mess we had got ourselves into!

Of course, it was difficult to complain about it because that, would give an indication that catching criminals automatically involved some wrongdoing. That would be a wrong perception because what it did, automatically changed what used to be man to man (or man to woman) chats between detectives and their suspects. These 'chats' would be conducted by good detectives using the same language of the suspect sat in front of them. They probably included many other topics not always connected with the crime for which they had been arrested. Matters possibly about their associates and other local crime, all subjects which would be aimed loosely as intelligence gathering which neither the detective or the suspect would want to be heard on a tape recorder or witnessed on CCTV.

It must be remembered that most of those suspects were very well-known to the police operating in city and county towns. Their families would also be known and it was not impossible for many generations of the same families to have been dealt with by the same detectives. The actual process of the interviews was not always a cut throat business. Many were not exactly cosy chats and there was little fear shown on either side. More often than not, the atmosphere would either be friendly but if not, time needed to be spent on getting it friendly.

Suspects were obviously found in tight corners and were concerned at the outcome of the predicament and what their fate might be. They needed to be turned to be able to trust you and occasionally, I have known interviews terminated after a confession and the shaking of hands. Putting everything on CCTV and a recording machine, put a stop to all that. Those law makers had done a fine job in tightening procedures, but they never realised that in addition to stamping out corruption, their measures would considerably result with more crime being committed and more criminals escaping justice. No longer were interview skills necessary and no longer would police be interested in the art of extracting 'coughs'.

Although just prior to my retirement I had used my powers to extend the periods of time suspects were allowed to remain in custody, these were the first duties I had performed under this fresh legislation. I was certainly not aware that as time slid by when PACE was in operation, that police officers were no longer responding to invitations to join the CID. As already stated, there had always been a queue of likely officers wanting to get their feet into the CID office. I could not believe that detectives were now shunning their jobs because they were now asking - "What's the point" and "It's never worth it".

We now have an abundance of TV 'fly on the wall' documentaries concerning the successful prosecution of those who have committed heinous offences. This has portrayed the fact that without forensic evidence such as fingerprints, DNA, CCTV, digital technology such as mobile phone forensics, computer technology, and automatic number plate readers etc., there would not be a chance of detecting such offences without such technological advances.

181

The skills of interviewing and the footslogging of evidence gathering techniques were all the tools that we had available, and which called for a good understanding of the types of criminals we were dealing with. These skills are now redundant but with the restrictions now imposed on the police, the use of the technologies now available, calls for different skills to be applied in the way evidence is gathered and used. In place of a cosy chat which would eventually get around to the suspect 'coughing' or not, a very good interview plan is now required even in the knowledge that the suspect is more than likely not going to make any comment about what is asked. But the interviewing police officers will still be required to give their evidence in contested cases which of course, will contain the questions they asked. This will now become the skill in conveying to juries, what it is that the police wanted to adduce in their questions which hopefully, would lead to their own presumptions.

I drool just by imagining how more successful we would have been in our day, if all those aids were available then. All I can say is, "WOW". It seems that resulting from police 'corrupt practice' we have now sat back and witnessed the changes, one after the other which in every case, have obstructed the paths of justice in the roles played by investigating police officers who hitherto, enjoyed catching criminals. For the number of crimes corrupt practise might have been detected, there will have since been far more committed by those more freely able to commit them without being captured.

Working at the 'Police Inspectorate' at the time, I was also aware that the CPS's remit included the objective of de-cluttering our courts with some borderline cases not seen viable to prosecute in the first place. I can concur that on many occasions, I had authorised proceedings for some cases which contained some element of doubt. Some I would not support going to court at all, but when I considered that the line between being guilty and innocent was very fine, I would mark files up with "Let the court decide", then give my reasons.

I can also agree that not infrequently, those summoned for cases such as 'Driving without Due Care and Attention' could take up a whole half day and more to be heard to their conclusion. So, perhaps justifiably, the CPS would not now proceed with them. Certainly, we would all be content to leave blame to the insurance companies involved.

But most importantly, if the CPS at first supported proceedings, they were empowered to later withdraw them or discontinue the process if that had already commenced. They would obviously discontinue cases when some 'not guilty' pleas were indicated if, on second thought, it became remotely likely that a not guilty plea would succeed. In other words, they would sooner side with the defendant than any prosecution case.

I felt that this was a form of waving the white flag saying in effect, "Ok, we've reconsidered and do not want to put up a fight. Do not bother to come to court, we concede". That power was obviously designed to save court time, but the sad thing about it is, that those hitherto contested cases would be heard when there were no waiting lists in being which were clogging up the system and more often than not, those borderline cases concluded in 'guilty' verdicts.

But the question must surely be asked, "what does this mean in the context of the criminal justice system and law breaking"? It was simply because the justice system is unable to cope, that people accused and processed to be prosecuted were now being 'let off', due to our courts and the prisons not being in a fit state to cope. A proportion of them I agree, will have been found not guilty but how many of the guilty would have escaped justice? Maybe it was a matter of coincidence but my fears that perverse decisions were made to 'short cut' the natural flow of justice were corroborated by many circumstances just one of which I experienced as follows: -

It was nineteen years ago when in May 2003, I was asked by West Mercia Police to review the cases being passed from the Redditch Criminal Support Unit (CJSU) to the CPS. Many had been rejected and my job was to review the quality of them which in many instances, was unbelievably poor. It was during this process that some files were being returned by the CPS with instructions not to proceed to a prosecution. There were many of these which I regarded as being very wrong decisions.

I could give many examples but uppermost in my mind after all these years have passed, concerned a young couple falling out over money issues. Because he was so upset, the husband drew many £50 notes out of the bank, got drunk and drove his wife's car into the shop front of the hairdressing salon in which she worked. He decamped and was later found at their home, still in a drunken state. He had ripped up some £50 notes leaving some pieces of them in the car, other pieces of them were found in his possession, together with his wife's car keys. He had been charged with the taking of his wife's car without consent, and all the 'drink drive' offences involved. His wife wanted rid of him and fully supported the prosecution. To cut a detailed story very short, not to include all the whys and wherefores, the CPS had decided that as there was no evidence from anyone witnessing him driving the car, they would not prosecute him. I wrote to the Chief Prosecuting Officer with a copy of the file containing the decision. To again cut this story short, the defendant ended up in court and was convicted. It did not take long for suspects to realise that they had what they might have considered 'friends' in the CPS who might not support the police's desire to have them charged. It does not take a brain surgeon to realise that unless they confess to the police, their chances of escaping justice had now increased by the erection of this obstacle between the police and themselves. There had to be a watertight case to proceed and no longer were cases ever left to 'let the court decide'.

This has not only caused the pendulum of justice to be swung too far in the criminal's favour but in fiscal terms, I merely add that in 2013, the CPS had an annual budget of over £590m. I can now understand why officers do not now want to join the CID. They would ask themselves, "what for"?

19. Police and Crime Commissioners

With hand on heart, I can honestly say that whichever political party police officers personally favoured, we acted in furtherance of the oath we took when we joined. I am also sure that our Chief Officers of Police were not, in any way swayed other than to protect the peace and catch law breakers. If they had been, then the message was not fed down to us at the coal face.

That situation was to change with the election of the Conservative / Liberal coalition in 2010. The government quite clearly were under the impression that chief constables were too autonomous; of could there be another reason why they wanted to introduce someone to oversee them? Chief Constables were indeed, almost totally autonomous and having worked close to the Home Office and many Chief Constables, I knew how the cog wheels slowly turned and I can imagine what the thinking process of government was. Legislation dictated that policing should be free from politics but of course, it is the politicians that in effect, make the laws.

Police budgets were funded mostly by the Home Office whose only control was exercised by the employment of HM Inspectors of Constabulary through annual inspections. We had a free hand to examine what we thought was pertinent, but the Home Office also issued us with the topics they wanted to be explored. But this process only took a few weeks a year and by no means was an all singing and dancing inspection. It would have been thought by the Home Office to have been far too light and maybe ineffective. In that context, I was once accompanied for a whole two weeks by a senior member of the 'Police Efficiency Unit' of the Home Office whilst conducting a pre inspection of a police force.

So, in a nutshell and for whatever reason, the Home Office must have considered that chief constables needed another more independent layer of local control. It is now history that they succeeded in that control by the introduction of directly elected individuals, who would be subject of checks and balances by local elected representatives. So having now dealt with the introduction of additional legislative measures concerning various police procedures and practices in the late 1980s, a further bolt from the blue suddenly hit the police service in 2012 through the passing of the Police Reform and Social Responsibility Act 2011 with the introduction of Police and Crime Commissioners to the English and Welsh police forces.

Of the relatively small number of changes made to the administration of the police witnessed since 1829, this was to be the most far-reaching step which I contend, apart from the effect on police chiefs, will have made little or no differences at all, other than it required quite heavy increases in the police budgets to pay for them.

The Police Act 1964 was the last of few modern-day statutes affecting the police service which, in addition to awarding pay rises, also introduced major reforms to the organisation and oversight of the police in England and Wales. It abolished the old watch committees for favour of independent 'Police Authorities' consisting of two thirds County Councillors and one third local magistrates. The remaining 'Borough Forces' were abolished by the Local Government Act 1972.

Typically, a police authority was made up of seventeen members consisting of nine elected members drawn from local authorities which would be reflective of the political makeup of them. The remaining eight members were called independent members and were appointed from the local community for fixed terms of four years by the police authority itself. It was these changes which possibly saw the thin edge of the wedge introducing the first signs of some real political control of the police.

At around the time of my retirement in 1994, the Government grant amounted to 51% of the budget with the rest coming from local authorities. This always brought consternation from the poorer, mainly agricultural counties because with limited incomes at their disposal, their 49% amounted to far less pro rata than the income derived from those richer manufacturing urban counties. But at least, the constitution of all police authorities provided a representation from all the areas being policed.

It must be said that the relationship with Chief Officers of Police and their Police Authorities was with few exceptions, a rather 'cosy' affair with business meetings taking place during heavy lunches, and so, it may well have been the case that this constitution was viewed by the Government of the day, to be far too 'cosy' and viewed as being ripe for a little extra political interference and control. However, in that context, suspicion that this was to become the thin edge of a wedge was raised only a few years later as will be explained a little later.

The new System

I think it fair to say, that what transpired in 2012, happened so stealthily and appeared so fast, that it took the service, and I am sure the public, completely by surprise. The appointment of Police and Crime Commissioners (PCCs) to oversee the activities of Chief constables and the police service they were providing, appeared to have been slid between the ribs of police forces, almost overnight.

The government however, had made a statement in 2010 that: "We will introduce measures to make the police more accountable through oversight by a directly elected individual, who will be subject to strict checks and balances by locally elected representatives". We had been warned, but unfortunately, amid an air of disbelief, not a lot of notice was taken of it beyond the top landings of police forces.

What could not be understood was, as explained above, that the police authorities to be replaced, consisted of representatives from all areas of the force. They were to be replaced by one person who more than likely would only know a fraction of the force area consisting, in West Mercia's case as an example, of three large counties. In addition, that one person had the power to hire and fire their chief constables.

Some of the applicants for the post lobbied under 'independent' banners but most had been aligned to political parties, many serving within their own local authorities, and they were often from a 'political' background and who had lived and worked in one small area of the force.

The first PCCs were elected in November 2012 and their responsibilities were about the same as their predecessor 'Police Authorities'. They became in theory only, the voice of the people and were to hold the police to account, were responsible for the totality of policing with an aim to cut crime and deliver an effective and efficient police service within their force area.

The one huge difference here, is that this one person, would not be replacing chief constables but they were to be responsible for holding chief constables and their forces to account, effectively making the police answerable to the communities they serve. This is exactly what Police Authorities did except that they were remote bodies of people, unpaid civil servants who were not present on a day-to-day basis, watching over the shoulder of the chief constable and his command team. The upshot being that control of police forces was strengthened but at the expense of severely weakening the community links with the people.

The following, which has been copy / pasted from the Government's GOV.UK Website makes their responsibilities very clear: -

Contact your police and crime commissioner (PCC) to make a suggestion or a complaint about how your local area is policed.

PCCs are elected in areas of England and Wales to make sure that local police meet the needs of the community. They are responsible for:

- *how your area is policed*

- *the police budget*

- *the amount of Council Tax charged for the police*

- *the information you get about what the local police are doing*

- *appointing and dismissing the chief constable (the most senior police officer for the area)*

Reading those responsibilities, one could be forgiven for believing that commissioners would be replacing chief constables. It is here that once again, I must apologise to the West Mercia Police and its PCC, John Campion for exampling them within this book but I am sure that their organisation and structure and the ethos they advertise and portray, will be very similar in all the other police force areas in England and Wales.

I can assure them that I completely respect them as individuals which in total make up the 'Force' and what has since become its PCC's organisation. In addition to my local knowledge of the area, I can gain an excellent insight through accessing their website and to do that in every one of the English and Welsh police forces would simply be impractical. My only aim is to do whatever I can to have our police forces and their members, regain their fine reputation, their respect, and the level of competency they once enjoyed.

So, with each force headquarters now being occupied with two sets of organisations charged with very much the same responsibility, the first question asked about this new organisation, begged the answer to the question, "Who was in charge of the Police Force"? Is it the chief constable or the PCC?

Despite what might be believed from those responsibilities and even with the appointment of these politicians witnessing the death of our previous independence from politics, every police force continues to operate with their same organisation and structures and with their chief constables continuing to be in operational command of their forces.

This was a heavy clue that the presence of PCCs were much to do with monitoring the operational efficiency of the force to see if it complied with what they were there to do.

The following statement by John Campion has been extracted from West Mercia's Policing Charter: -

Police and Crime Commissioner John Campion said: "Keeping the community at the heart of policing has always been my priority as Commissioner. As police officer numbers rise, it is right we are able to see measurable impact in our communities.

"It is clear from community feedback that the force needs to continue to build a strong, visible presence, with communities able to access officers when they

need to. I will work with the Chief Constable to ensure service improvements are delivered alongside the best possible return for the public's investment, this charter is a big step in that happening."

Here! here! Mr Campion. We are both singing off the same hymn sheet and I sincerely wish that you will achieve the goals you have set. I had of course, retired but I would have loved to learn how the chiefs and their commissioners played out their individual roles now that they were almost doing the same job. However, as the nation has now witnessed on many occasions, we now have PCCs putting forward details and objectives of operational policing on nationwide media.

Under Police Regulations 2003, Regulation 11, chief constables can be offered a contract for five years in the first instance, followed by a further three years, and thereafter a 12-month contract. There is no limit to the number of one-year contracts that can be offered thereafter.

The huge disadvantage of having this almost dual command, is I contend, that they can in effect, silence each other whereby chief constables will not wish to upset their PCCs for fear of not having their contracts renewed and PCCs will be in similar positions every time they present themselves at ballot boxes to continue their role. In that vein, they will not be wishing to upset their chief constables for fear of them muddying the waters at least, at their election time. If that is not happening, then surely it means that both are very happy about the other's organisation? If so, what was the object of foisting this additional layer of bureaucracy into Police Headquarters? Chief Constables all have quite large management teams consisting of a Deputy, two or more Assistant Chief Constables and a plethora of support staff at senior levels, in addition to the commanders of every command unit in the force. Why then is there any need for this additional very costly layer of management?

Gone are the days when we could hear voices of Chief Constables such as James Anderton of the Greater Manchester Police who was known as the 'Coppers' Cop', resounding off the walls of the Home Office calling for whatever he thought would enhance the quality of policing, whether that be resources for his own force or simply support for the police service in general.

There are now no such voices so far as I am aware and Chiefs have their commissioners sitting on their proverbial shoulders ensuring that they are compliant with their wishes and although I have no evidence to the contrary, I suspect that it is they, who will have a direct line of communications to the Home Office as the **'spy** on the wall' at police headquarters.

But the even larger dilemma concerns the question about having this additional tier of policing management which when it boils down to it, produces objectives which are almost identical to that of what is or would be expected to be produced by most chief constables. It is hard to think of an analogy but a bit like blasting vermin at point blank range with one barrel of a shot gun and then doing the same with the other barrel for the hell of it.

So, amid this utter confusion, I return to the question I posed above, "What was the object of foisting this additional layer of bureaucracy into Police Headquarters?" It wasn't until after this book had been proofread and indeed loaded on Amazon ready for publication, that I came upon a government Consultation paper dated September 2015 and headed, 'Enabling closer working between the emergency services'. I had already become surprised when I had earlier discovered that the Police Inspectorate had now been merged with that of the Fire and Rescue Inspectorate. I was also aware that the local Police and Crime Commissioner was to operate in a similar role with the local Fire and Rescue service, as he had been operating with regard to the police. I may well have been slow on the uptake other than a passing belief that the suspected rationale was a cost saving measure but as strange as it seems now, it wasn't until I discovered this Government 'Consultation' paper that the intended breadth of the Police and Crime Commissioner's responsibilities of the future, had not been completely understood by me and I guessed, had not been understood by the vast majority of our population.

The enthusiasm and insignificance of the whole subject was probably reflected in there being an average of only 15% turnout of the 2012 electorate (14.6% in West Mercia). In West Mercia, two of the three candidates were respectively proposed by the Conservative and Labour parties and the third lobbied under the banner of 'Independent'. Indeed, it was as if the electorate wanted to shun the politicians, that they voted in the 'Independent' who happened to be a retired police superintendent! Yes, a retired superintendent with the power now, to sack the chief constable?

But now it appears to me that to have issued this consultation paper in September 2015, those at the Home Office working on it must have taken several years to get to its publication. Surely, they must have been working on this during the time that PCCs were being appointed. If this plan had been known at that time, those of us who couldn't understand the wisdom or purpose of their appointments would surely have then become aware that there was a far longer term plan involved in the birth of our PCCs. That is very much confirmed by the consultation paper in that the intended outcome would be that they would head the organisations evolving from the plan to merge the three emergency services. Surely this was the early plans for a cloak and dagger operation which was to strengthen central government's control of our police, fire, and ambulance services?

One might have expected that the PCC's organisations would grow but I had already pointed out in this book that an absolute fortune is now being expended on this organisation, without as far as I can see, no improvement in the policing of our communities. Much to the contrary. The payment of the police grant to the old Police Authorities was to operate the same with the new PCCs. The structure of it in West Mercia is bound to be like that elsewhere but so far as West Mercia was concerned, there are now 25 members of staff holding positions employed under the following described titles. Please read them all as they will provide loose pictures as to what is involved: -

Chief Executive, Head of Youth Justice Service, Head of Estates, Treasurer, Finance Officer x 2, Head of Communications and Engagement, Senior Communications and Engagement Officer, Communications Officer, Estates Communications Officer, Digital Communications and Engagement Assistant, Casework Officer, Personal Assistant to the PCC, Personal Assistant to the Deputy and Assistant PCCs, Personal Assistant to the CEO, Treasurer and Head of Policy and Commissioning, Head of Policy and Commissioning, Senior Commissioning Officer, Senior Policy Officer, Commissioning Officer, Commissioning Assistant, Sexual Violence Portfolio Lead, Policy Officer x 2, Co-

ordinator for the PCCs Independent Custody Visitors' Scheme, Policy and Commissioning Intern.

Force personnel

In addition, the PCC's Staff Officer post is a police sergeant on a secondment from West Mercia Police.

Also, several support services provided under the direction and control of the chief constable are made available to the Commissioner when required. A memorandum of understanding sets out these services.

Local authority personnel

Internal audit and payroll services are provided by Worcestershire County Council.

Complaints review function which is undertaken by an independent qualified external body.

Whilst a more detailed description of each post holder can be found by visiting the PCCs website *(https://www.westmercia-pcc.gov.uk/your-pcc/pcc-team/)* one merely has to read the description of each post to realise what a massive organisation has sprung from nowhere to append itself upon our already overworked police service which appears to be less efficient as each year turns.

This situation is compounded by the fact that commissioners can issue a precept, thus allowing council tax to be levied in order to fund themselves, in addition to the police. This of course, means that we are paying thousands, if not millions of pounds to feed this monster, yet we see a decline in our police services. By contrast, I suspect that nothing much more than a quarterly lunch would amount to the expense incurred for the old Police Authorities. The method in the madness is perhaps becoming clearer.

So, we appear to have been landed with a brand-new layer of bureaucracy built into the 'top landing' of police headquarters which now must be bursting at the seams with this vast new group of personnel which appears to be treading in the same water as all the problems which the force had hitherto been swimming in. This might be a 'shallow' appreciation, but it is what most people believe.

The communities policed, were also suffering from those making their lives even more miserable by our ever expanding 'law breaking' sections of society and this new organisation was never going to make any difference. There appears to be no 'pay back' received because of this 'elephant in the room' intrusion and I can find no-one who has argued otherwise.

I agree that there should be some meaningful level of accountability over the police and that it should possibly contain more teeth than possessed by our old Police Authority. The organisation and structure of it being so widespread was ideal. But I contend that what it lacked, was maybe one or two, say the Chairman and Vice Chairman being paid members of it and employed at the centre with the other local authority members feeding into that centre, the trials, and tribulations of their respective communities.

Apart from a personal assistant / secretary, he or she or 'they' would be able to use the same administrative resources as the chief constable. The same objective could remain, but such an organisation would ensure that the independency of the authority would once again be spread all over the force area. But all this would not, of course assist the government in what now appears could well have been their hidden agenda for the PCC concept.

So, not withstanding, now let us look in more detail of what emanates from those PCC organisations. We could be forgiven for believing that we have been fed with the same gobbledegook promises, policies and threats as have been experiences by that of our police forces. Having studied the contents of Mr Campions' web site, I could be left with the impression that his organisation is just an adjunct to the West Mercia Police, the Chief Constable and his force. I realise that it would be a plus if both worked side by side in the policing operation but surely that was not the intention? The PCCs were asked to ensure that chief constables were carrying out their duties satisfactorily not duplicating them at such a cost.

The below is the first banner I came across when I examined PCC John Campion's opening gambit. I believe it says a great deal of what he believes is his role, especially if my suspicions regarding the extreme widening of his and other PCC's responsibilities in the future are correct.

First, the Conservative Party 'tree' logo just serves to underline the fact that here we have a political champion in Mr Campion (no pun intended)

Then, the 'My plan to cut crime further' link positioned in the top left-hand corner bewilders me because surely any plan to cut crime is a matter beneath the operational command of the chief constable? In my view, if the PCC considers that the Chief was failing in that respect, then, on behalf of the communities he serves, it would be his duty to tell him so and to ensure that something is done about it. Maybe his statement goes to prove that they duplicate each other.

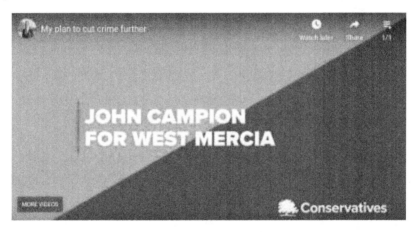

I have listened to Mr Campions speech in this link and not surprisingly, most of his words are those what are expected of him. However, I can find nothing which convinces me that he and his organisation have carried out the plans intended for them. They should be the link with the communities of the three counties. Have they received any complaints about policing and if so, what was done about it? That would be their remit as far as I am aware.

I was particularly bewildered at him giving his assurance that communities will have embedded police teams at their heart and that they would be accessible to the communities. Yet, with also mentioning that they have employed an additional 400 police officers since 2016, finding a police officer on beat patrol or getting one to respond to an incident or answer a telephone call, appears to be the main concern of their communities.

And of course, the closure of police stations will do nothing to help him ensure that the position will improve. With the remit given to PCCs, this becomes another area where more positive steps could be taken to improve policing.

He claims that increased technical resources have been responsible for the fall in crime. His assumption though, is that things would have stood still without them. On the one hand, without the police being present to police the community, less crime has been reported for a long time because of the reasons detailed in the chapters above. West Mercia Police had always been among the top of performing forces and we were so proud of that because we were also among the poorest. We are now among the worst performing and were placed in the equivalent of 'special measures.' But again, I do not wish to use West Mercia as a measuring stick because there will still be many other good and poor performing forces.

It was, pleasing however, that although his 'Safer West Mercia Plan' is quite long and contained all that which you could expect he would say, it was written in plain English with little signs of the gobbledegook associated with the policy documents and objectives written within the police service. However, the cost of building the commissioner's teams must have detracted from that previously provided to Police Authorities but much more could be achieved if their total budgets were now released towards the sharp end of policing as opposed to supporting their huge organisations.

20. Recruitment and Training

The methods of recruiting and training our police will have experienced various changes throughout the past decades and probably go hand in hand with our changing societies and values. As I have said previously, in my era of the 1960s, it was just necessary to complete a pro-forma application form and if you met the physical requirements and passed a few simple tests in spelling, arithmetic and general knowledge, then you were recruited or maybe if you could represent the force in any of the force's sporting pursuits, you were in anyway.

The Police Staff College at Bramshill was in operation and progression to senior command was gained through an accelerated promotion scheme to sergeant via the 'Special Course' and the attendance there of officers completing command courses, the 'Senior Command' course for the highest NPCC ranks. At the other end of the scale, recruits were trained generally for thirteen weeks at several District Police Training Centres.

I do not think that a lot changed in the general recruitment and training world until maybe the late 1980s when the 'Student Instructors' course lasting about ten weeks was required to be re-written and for a start, the term 'police instructor' was to be replaced with 'police trainer'. I suspect that that made a whole lot of difference to those being taught – or maybe not?

This was the era when the old fashioned 'chalk and talk' method of teaching was dropped to be replaced by a complete change of style which entailed more of a 'forum' style of tuition involving an 'open discussion' designed to cause relevant information to be processed. This new method had sarcastically been referred to as 'beanbag learning', depicting students sat on beanbags whilst discussing maybe, the elements of crimes to identify whether a particular set of circumstances given, amounted to a particular crime. It was obviously hoped that the discussion would remain with the students so that forever more, they would be assisted in making up their own minds as to whether offences had been committed.

Also, no longer was it necessary for recruits to suffer the same level of discipline as hitherto experienced by those of the past. We were all pals together and as a bonus, there was no requirement now to learn parrot fashion, all those dreaded police definitions of the numerous crimes we might come across.

I had not experienced this myself and so, doubting that such debate would be more effective, the following is a selection of replies I received on our West Mercia Memories 'Face Book' site: -

Tim Higgs

I became a trainer in the late 1980s, the system had just changed, we were called 'trainers' as opposed to 'Instructors'. We were also called 'tree huggers' by some of those who went through the old school. There was no requirement to learn any definition by that time.

Simon Newton-Smith

I joined in 1969 just as the Theft Act and Road Safety Acts had been implemented, so not only did I know all my definitions as a young probationer I was helping more established officers with the new law. That was in Bristol.

As an inspector at Telford, I was one of the first to go to the new 'trainers' courses, 10 weeks if I remember correctly and I think it was around 1988. It was quite a transitional and difficult period as the first 'graduates' were saying that the old methods were wrong, and this did not go down well.

I was the only inspector in the class, the majority were constables or sergeants. Our trainer, for just 4 weeks, was a traditionalist. So, he insisted on being called "Sir" except for me and I could call him by his first name. So, there was a dilemma what should my classmates call me …. I finished up as 'Sir Simon'.

No mention of definitions was made at that time.

Robin Evans

I did a Student Instructors Course at Pannal Ash in 1985. In January 1987, John Williams and I were PC instructors and did what was called a 'Trainers Development' course – run for all Student Instructors trained to become 'facilitators'. As you suggested, this introduced the ethos of 'experiential' student-based learning based on research by I think the University of East Anglia. I left the training school at Droitwich on promotion to sergeant later that year grateful that learning of definitions served me well.

Neil Manson

"I joined back end of 1987. No parrot learning of definitions then. And so, it seems that the 1987-8 period was when things began to change."

I am obviously going to favour the old school method but only because that was how I was taught though having reviewed constables' crime enquiries during my REP phase of reviewing them, I was very satisfied that not many understood the elements of the crimes which needed to be proved, nor did their supervisors. I am sure others trained in what was then, the new system will favour that system, but that's just life! They were familiar with it as it was the only system they knew. However, the below was submitted by Tim Burling which might help those sitting on the fence to make up their minds: -

> *I Joined in 1989. Remember sitting around discussing how we interpreted aggravated burglary instead of actually teaching us what it was. Guess what, none of us understood it until one of the training Inspectors chucked out the beanbags and sat us behind desks and actually taught us what it meant, ordering us to learn the definition verbatim. Up to that point we had not been instructed to learn definitions. Once it had been taught properly instead of us just working out what we thought it meant, it was easy. I started to learn definitions off my own bat after that. The sitting around in a circle on metaphorical beanbags was clearly not the answer to police training.*

When working in the 'Retired Experienced Personnel' scheme, I had been asked to review the recorded crimes and how they were being investigated by trawling the new 'CRIMES' computer system. I discovered a dreadful slump in the overall recording and investigation of them so my overall objective was to highlight what could be responsible for this dip. I have already explained in chapters past that I concluded that it was tantamount to the 'blind leading the blind'.

What does really concern me now, is the subject I have earlier touched upon and which concerns the very recent changes in recruitment that have now appeared to have completely negated the concept of the force being a microcosm of society. I reproduce below, that which I have copied and pasted from the West Mercia Police Website in their quest for more recruits.

Their advertisements are exactly what has now very recently been encouraged by The Home Office and promulgated by the College of Policing. I have included just a paragraph or two which describes the headings: -

Police Constable Degree Apprenticeships

Work as a full time police officer and gain a recognised degree

As a Police Constable Degree Apprentice, you'll be working as a full time police officer, earning a starting salary of £24,219 and learning crucial skills to become a fully qualified officer. You'll also gain a paid-for degree level qualification on the job from Staffordshire University in Professional Policing Practice.

Degree Holder Entry Programme

Work as a full time police officer and gain a recognised Graduate Diploma in Professional Policing Practice.

As a fulltime student police officer, you will be able to build upon the degree you have already gained, earning a starting salary of £25,269 (rising to £30,060 within 5 years) whilst learning the skills to become a fully qualified police officer.

Detective Constable Entry Routes

Join West Mercia Police and become a detective.

Working as a detective constable is one of the most demanding, but also rewarding roles in Policing. You will make West Mercia a safer place to live and work, protecting people from harm and providing the best outcomes for victims and their families.

Professional Policing Degree

We are now recruiting for new police officers to join West Mercia's Professional Policing Degree (PPD) Programme.

The PPD programme is the route into Policing for graduates with a degree in Professional Policing. This route is sometimes called 'Pre-Join'.

This situation worries me because I know very well through my own experiences that our numbers should include that microcosm of society with as many of them as possible, possessing an abundance of common sense. The above-described methods of recruiting, flies directly into the face of that concept and we were always proud of the fact that we policed with the consent of the community. That will no longer apply to be true if the recruits are now to be found from those above-described channels.

I generalise of course, but whether the average level of education possessed by the communities of today is higher or lower, by and large, the people who the police most deal with in our communities, are not degree holders and thus do not anywhere near possess that level of education.

The term that the police have now become the 'dustbin of our society' is not far from being accurate. Indeed, although most degree holders will be able to adapt, they will be more likely to 'get up the noses' of those being dealt with rather than the boys and girls who were by some margin closer to themselves.

Those types I am thinking of are in fact those without a degree who will make good detectives and who will not be keen to join with a view to study for one. Their potential supervisors would prefer them to be performing general police duties prior to entering the CID. This would ensure that they possess an aptitude to become CID officers. Believe me, they are in the minority, so how are they to be identified when they join the CID as 'direct entry' recruits? It is those which demonstrate their aptitude for CID work who are the types who have an abundance of common sense and the nous to be able relate to their future 'clients'.

In addition, should recruitment forge ahead without taking this heed, what will be the position when most all young officers will comprise degree holders? In general terms, I agree that the appointment of higher educationally qualified in the command posts would be most suitable but however, I can always remember the quote heard from many – **"We seem to have more Chiefs than Indians"** being appropriate should that situation pertain. That would cause frustration and resentment. Daggers would be drawn!

In my humble estimation, and without using that popular description 'evidence based' which one day, I shall threaten to call out and see what evidence really does exist, I argue that if the PCSO concept could be expanded so that they could perform those tasks previously performed by beat officers, then that could so easily be the first step which might re-set that concept which actually did cause to prove that it was most effective and efficient and indeed was 'Community Policing'.

Just quickly adding to my view of the over used and unnecessary 'evidence based' term mentioned above, does it mean that good fresh ideas cannot now be explored these days without prior evidence being used or that the absence of the term means that lessons learned in the past were only those which were tried and failed? Anyway, I have drifted from the subject of the recruitment of a more educated police service and the well-worn terms: -

1. We need the consent of the community to police the community and

2. We receive the policing we deserve.

I contend that such changes will only help to alienate even further, the community from its police. Most of whom the police deal with at local street level are the types that despise 'degree holder' types who will be identified with ease. Bobbies on the beat score by being able to talk to these people at their level and not by putting on an act of superiority.

In addition, frustration will be felt by those graduates who, the majority of which will soon realise that they cannot all be chiefs. Many of the colleagues under my supervision in the lowest of ranks regularly told me that they were too happy in the constable rank to even seek promotion. I just cannot see a host of graduates accepting that stance.

Bearing in mind the views I have already expressed about the over inclusion of 'Wokism' as an ideology among our police service, what worries me even more is the publication of a book I discovered during my research into these new avenues of recruitment to our forces titled: -

Police Education in the United Kingdom: Challenges and Future Directions

This book appears to be the Bible of future recruitment to the police. It has been compiled by the following four academics - criminologists, education experts and general high-ranking academics and was published on 17th August 2022. (Not many months ago)

All but Mr Julian Parker-McLeod hold PhD Doctorates. A brief Google search of them reveals more clearly who they are-

M. Mahruf C. Shohel

Dr M. Mahruf C. Shohel is currently working at the University of Roehampton, United Kingdom. Prior to this role, Dr Shohel worked for several British universities since he completed his doctoral studies at the University of Manchester.

He is an academic researcher and educationalist with special interests in education, childhood studies, international development, teachers' professional development, technology-enhanced learning, and social science research methods. Most recently, he has taught 'Digital Learning in Emergencies" for postgraduates at the University of Geneva, Switzerland.

He has written extensively on development issues in the Global South and conducted research on disadvantaged children including socioeconomically deprived children, street children, sex workers' children, and displaced refugee children. Currently, Dr Shohel is engaged in the fields of education in emergencies, education for sustainable development and global citizenship, emerging technologies in education, students\' learning journeys, student engagement, and teaching and learning in higher education.

Dr Gias Uddin Ahmed is a poet, journalist and researcher. He felt it important to compile a book about the ancient and modern history of universities. Once upon a time we knew, and believed that the Al Hazler Alighar Muslim and Madina University were famous universities. Also, the Dhaka University is the Oxford of eastern world.

Dr. Gias Uddin Ahmed

We feel proud of the civilianisation of Egypt, Babylonian and Athens. But we are aware and do not learn more about the Sind civilianisation of ancient India. But nowadays, Middle East, Africa and many other countries of Asia the education system is not; compared to the modern world. According to the world ranking many universities are uncountable. He says that his book will be helpful for those who are interested to know the roots of the higher education system.

Mr. Julian Parker-McLeod (No photograph)

Julian Parker-McLeod is the Director of Professional Education Programmes, at the Faculty of Humanities and Social Sciences, School of Criminology and Criminal Justice.

Dr. Daniel Silverstone

He quotes "The tragic death of George Floyd while in the custody of officers from the Minneapolis police department in US highlights the differences between US and UK policing but a common issue is the under representation of black and minority ethnic (BAME) in their ranks. Dr Daniel Silverstone and Dominique Walker from Liverpool John Moores University discuss the progress of improving diversity in UK policing."

Even though I have no plans to read this book, I worry about what its contents might contain if, as I suspect, that police practitioners have not contributed to it. In any event, it will be loaded from this academia stance. The book was published under reference (DOI: 10.5772/intechopen.92705) by IntechOpen with, I believe, an objective to explain in more depth, the three newly introduced routes for recruitment and education of constables under the Policing Educations Framework (PEQF) as described above.

There is an accompanying note which says – 'Part of the book: Education, Human Rights and Peace in a Sustainable Development'.

The buzz word 'Sustainable' frightens me because I have noticed that it recently tends to be used as an adjective in just about every description of a writer's topic where the author needs to bolster up the noun being referred to. In other words, it is overused just like 'evidenced based' and 'holistic' and all those currently fashionable buzz words and phrases used by many who write 'gobbledegook' as a preferred language.

The four academic experts described above are obviously at the top of their various trees in the world of academia. It is the ensuing system and influence of what I would describe as a misguided 'College of Policing' trend coupled with Home Office officials who have very little experience in the subjects they are promulgating but obviously hold their strong desires and influence to firm up and in their own minds, clean up the professionalism of policing. That might be required but let us not throw out the baby with the bath water. Where is the 'Police Input' to all the recommendations of this Policing Educations Framework (PEQF)?

It was as if salt was being rubbed into the wounds when I read in The Times dated 18th November 2022, it states quite clearly that the Quality Assurance Agency which reviews university teaching standards, has opened a new front in the great wokeness, urging academics in almost every field to promote the new orthodoxy. As an example, they quote maths tutors being encouraged to promote a multicultural and de-colonised view of Mathematics. It says that Biomedical scientists should tell students that their predecessors were guilty of misogyny, racism, homophobia, ableism (whatever that means) and other prejudices. It adds 'and even computer scientists ludicrously, should show that divisions and hierarchies of colonial value are replicated and reinforced within the computing subject'.

It is as if those horrible stories of bad policing which sadly, we have endured more of in these recent months and years have propelled their need to orbit police experts and have handed the sick baby over to the doctors (Ph.D. doctors of course).

Yes, I am all for equality for all, whether or not they belong to any gender or LGBT+ group and I am against sexism and racism but no, why our police recruits should be influenced by academic lecturers in anything but the learning of the police subjects being taught, I shall never know.

And in the very same newspaper, I read that an outgoing Oxford University vice chancellor has warned that some students (a minority) now believe that they have a right not to be offended by hearing the opposing views of their colleagues. I say again – **"HAS THE WORLD GONE MAD"?** and I only make that statement to emphasise the fact that we, our recruits, and trainers alike, should not be getting embroiled in any such nonsense which I may have misclassified as 'Woke' views.

21. Conclusions

Readers may recall my earlier comments concerning the Police Research and Scientific Development Branch of the Home Office spending two years in Kirby, Lancashire analysing the effects of Community Policing, and which concluded that the patrolling beat police officers had no real impact on crime and that they would be better served by a panda car patrol. It would be interesting now to ask them if, in hindsight, they were happy with the results of that experiment which produced what was officially known as 'Unit Beat Policing' and which I have described herein as 'Pizza Slice' policing. It came as no surprise therefore, that in January 2006, the Home Office Research, Development and Statistics Directorate published their findings of a twelve month analysis called 'An evaluation of the impact of the National Reassurance Policing Programme'. (NRPP) This was a similar analysis over a 12-month period at 16 locations.

Although much like interviewing suspects of crime these days, no admissions were made of the failure of the 1960s 'Unit Beat Policing' system. I have said many times in this book that whilst the reporting of crimes and their detection rates can be measured, the prevention of crime is impossible to measure. Yet for the second time, an attempt to measure the various aspects of crime was made, this time by the NRPP. The first paragraph of the FOREWORD to an extremely lengthy report provides a snapshot of the objective: -

> Neighbourhood policing has become a central part of the Government's police reform programme. The basis of a neighbourhood policing model is to have dedicated police resources for local areas and for police and their partners to work together with the public to understand and tackle the problems that matter to them most. International evidence had shown indications that this type of local policing could serve to reduce both actual and perceived levels of crime and disorder, as well as to improve the public's perceptions of the police. The development of a UK evidence base on the impact of this type of local policing activity is critical to the success of the reform programme and to sustained investment.

This research was conducted seventeen years ago! Clearly and perhaps understandably, the Home Office are unwilling to contribute public funds to projects without statistical data in terms of proving positive outcomes. Nevertheless, their positive comments under the headings 'Implications for Policy' and 'Implications for Practice' should be read. The report also states that there are no agreed estimates of costs available for anti-social behaviour, fear, confidence, and feelings of safety. This whole demand for evidential process continues to baffle me as to why such experiments in statistical terms are even attempted when cost savings cannot accurately be obtained. The data must lie within a shifting bed according to varying moods of the era and location, which I believe must surely indicate that the reliance on statistical data could never be accurately guaranteed. For example, I have indicated within this book, that the absence of neighbourhood policing will have affected the reporting of crime. In the absence of visibility and the difficulties often encountered in communicating with the police, injured parties often drawn the conclusion that 'What's the point'! A different story if the local bobby was 'on hand'.

As stated in my introduction, I realise that my views are my own drawn from my own experience and hence, they are arrived at without statistical evidence to support them. I contend that it is the people who reside on large housing estates or who are resident in more isolated rural areas who should simply be asked: -

"Would you prefer to be policed by any sort of presence locally or rely on police attendance in response to occurrences"?

I believe that I do not need to suggest what the answers would be.

So, I congratulate those who have reached this point. You will recall that I started this book on 9th September 2022, the day following the death of our Queen Elizabeth 11; that sad event, which was the cause of me writing this book. Christmas 2022 has now concluded, and this book is now in the hands of the proof-readers. Two Prime Ministers have been despatched and we are now on our third! Vladimir Putin is still shelling those poor people in the Ukraine, just about everyone is on strike and we have encountered Arctic weather. I listened to Radio 5 Live this morning when the debate was, "Is our country now broken"? I joined the debate by shouting at the radio but alas, no-one could hear me!

Although it was for the reasons stated on that first page, that stirred me into action, it has taken me this three month plus period to realise that it was much more than what the Queen might have felt about our criminality that taught me exactly what it was that had caused our slump in the value of community policing. I had a rough Idea, but it was not until then that I can now clearly see what the three main causes were: -

1. The visibility of and the communication with our community policing took a dive when we sold the police houses on those estates which ironically were built to get our beat officers closer to the communities. Owning our own houses had indirectly caused policing from central hubs and 'Fire Brigade' reactionary policing ensued. There were no preventive measures left.

2. With the loss of mature supervisors coinciding with a relaxing of discipline, the new generation of supervisors did not always match the expertise of those who had retired or otherwise left the force.

3. As commented on the pages immediately above this, The Police Research and Development Branch of the Home Office had spent over two years in researching the conventional methods of policing on the beat and they resolved that the uniform constable on it does no positive work against crime. I will not duplicate that said above but I implore the viewing of the short film at -
   https://www.youtube.com/watch?v=OLPjrhM4X-w

These three and a half months have failed to cheer me up to any extent, but I can declare that I am not that 'grumpy old git' as is described on the socks bought for me by a grandchild. I am indeed, a **VERY** grumpy old git! Our 'Justice System' has now joined the NHS and our 'Social Care' system for being well and truly broken. What with members of our communities not always bothering to report crimes, police not being able to detect so many of them as they used to, the backlog of court cases increasing and with our prisons being full to exploding, it just does not make any sense at all. The re-set lever must be pulled very quickly.

In this time of writing, I have been forced to make continuing insertions regarding the disastrous and terrible stories of the women who have suffered at the hands of two Metropolitan Police Officers. It will take years for the shadows those officers have caused to be cast on our police service to shift but they will remain if, in my view, the Metropolitan Police is not broken up. They have proved over and over again that policing appears far more effective and efficient when it occurs on the ground and not on wheels. My later experiences post amalgamation, also indicated to me that although more resources and opportunities were available, 'Big is not always Beautiful'. We did not, of course, have the crime case load as is the case nowadays but nevertheless, I would not advocate any further merges towards general community (local) policing which accounts for around 90% of policing activity.

However, it is clearly time for another re-set. Our digital world has now turned many, if not most crimes into being so national and internationally committed to make our 'local' police completely inadequate to deal with them. In those types of cases, as has happened with the inception of the Central Motorway Patrol Group (CMPG) for motorway policing, the same sort of regionalisation could and should be developed for tackling such crimes. But whatever, we must not continue to lose our local, community policing and resist at all costs, the temptation to merge forces. We must remember many of the failures we now suffer have been caused through cost cutting measures without considering long term effects.

I can now declare that the reason for my grumpiness is that my experiences in the police have embraced such a long period of time because I was lucky enough to have climbed far higher up that greasy pole than ever, I had imagined. I have been in the right places at the right times on many occasions and being the youngest in those ranks, my memory and experiences have been far wider and have extended beyond my warrant card holding days making my armoury of experiences far more extensive than most of my colleagues.

My research and reflections have now helped me arrive at a general conclusion that to cure ills, the wrong medication appears to have been prescribed. This has contributed to the death of policing within and with the community. Although the deceased's symptoms were slow to affect death, the coroner has declared the following to be included on the death certificate, in no order: -

1. Relaxing of the police regulations which provided Chief Officers the power to direct where his officers were to reside.
2. Selling the family silver consisting of police houses and village police stations.
3. Closing far too many urban police stations creating a more widespread use of 'reactive policing'.
4. The utilisation of community police officers in motor cars working from hubs and not in the community. (Giving up beat ownership)
5. The hypocrisy of advocating the need to police with a microcosm of society, when banning most of the community from being recruited without educational degrees or wanting to earn one as an apprentice. (Not yet a cause but should be viewed as a 'preventive measure' as for sure, it will be a further nail in the coffin if allowed to proceed.)
6. The Replacing of 'First Contact' trained police officers with civilian personnel without policing experience.
7. The general ill-discipline and criminal activities of police officers – 'Bent Coppers' and the resultant over prescribed measures, especially time constraints for holding suspects. The PACE act should be reviewed now that experiences have been learned and attitudes changed.
8. The need to review the effects case law has had concerning suspects exercising their right not to answer police questions. (No Comment)
9. The grading of calls to the police resulting in some requests for police attendance to be declined.
10. Poor leadership at ground level. (Sergeants in particular)
11. Poor leadership at top landings to identify it and introduce measures accordingly. (Education and Training – professionalism and leadership / management skills)
12. Allowing academia an over influence to dictate police training requirements.
13. Neglecting the core duties of police to prevent and detect crime, keep the peace, and apprehend offenders against the peace.
14. Killing off the concept of policing without political interference. (Review the need for PCCs and spend the money on needed resources)

15. The ineffectiveness of police to tackle modern fraudsters and cybercrime. Most will be unreported as public ask, "Why bother". These crimes are reported to all different forces, but offenders may well be in different countries. The banks and police should combine their resources in one centralised base to receive and investigate all of these crimes.
16. Replacing those core duties with an over emphasis on human resource matters not directly affecting them. (Taking eyes off the ball)
17. Ceasing to routinely deploy designated 'Crime Prevention' officers to burglaries where they could make a difference. However, I am told that to a certain extent, they have been replaced by DOCOs (Design Out Crime Officers.)

I feel convinced that it is the new generation of professional policing practice and study now evolving who have a great deal to do with the direction to be taken in this modern era of policing.

I mean by this, the leaders at the 'Police Department of the Home Office, the 'academia' of police research and the profession of policing itself such as through the National Police Chiefs Council, the College of Policing and the Police Inspectorate, right down to the lack of experienced operators and leaders at community policing level who, through no fault of their own, were not so employed when 'Community Policing' died. The corpse has now laid dead for so long that it is so decomposed that first aid and sticky plasters are rendered useless. Even scalpels are blunted. It is only a resurrection which we can hope will cause an effect.

Without a great deal of eating humble pie and a willingness to learn from the past, it will take giant leaps of faith and a huge amount of courage to get us back on the tracks of the most effective methods of community policing so that a firm platform can be utilised to work in conjunction with the more modern tools contained in today's policing armoury. We can put away any reliance on statistical analysis and just do it! We need to be quick because a general election is on the horizon, and all this may soon be forgotten after it!

22. About the Author

Brian and his wife Jo reside in a village close to Worcester. They have two married daughters living in the vicinity and four adult grandchildren, the eldest two both gaining first class honours degrees with the other two, yet to finalise their studies.

Brian's experience has been spread over so many aspects of policing which has more than qualified him for providing his opinions as to the reasons why community policing lies 'in state' today.

On retiring, he became involved as a self-employed contractor in the 'roll-out' of the first computerised fingerprint identification system in England and Wales and later in the Caribbean Islands. He also worked for an American software company based near Seattle, Washington State and as a para legal in a top USA firm of solicitors. (Preston Gates)

When his work abroad concluded in 2002, he became a private investigator and developed a Business Association on a crime infested Worcestershire Industrial Estate. His work led to the provision of substantial capital funds to help the estate's regeneration.

Whilst continuing his freelance work, he also became contracted by the West Mercia Constabulary's Deputy Chief Constable to provide a 'model' for the organisation and structure of the force's Personal Standards departments across the large force area. Being already computer literate prior to some forces incorporating personal computers for general use, this led him to be employed as a member of the West Mercia Constabulary's 'Retired Experienced Personnel' scheme. He assisted in the investigation of 'cold case' crimes and to review how crimes were then recorded and investigated by use of a new digital system.

He was also engaged in the training of officers in other 'Police Software' such as the new 'Missing Persons' system. Brian fully retired in 2009 having been the manager of a challenging senior school and now continues his genealogical hobbies which have involved him writing other 'social history' books. In addition, he continues playing golf, bowls, table tennis and croquet.

At home, he sometimes catches glimpses of his wife Jo who prefers him playing sports rather than "tap tap tapping on that computer all the time". Despite having lived in nine police houses in the past, they have defied the phrase, 'Join the Force and get a Divorce' and look forward to their diamond wedding anniversary in 2026.

Brian's previous books are related to his 'Family History' hobby and to the surrounding social history stories of times past. He won a prize for writing a story called 'My Family Hero' which was promoted by the 'Who Do You Think You Are? Magazine.

He has written a previous police based history book concerning his 46 years in the police family. His last book, 'Big Talk Murder at Birchen Coppice' concerned his interesting investigation into a 1981 murder committed on a council housing estate at Kidderminster, Worcestershire.

Printed in Great Britain
by Amazon

26699508R00119